DELICIOUS MEMORIES

DELICIOUS MEMORIES

RECIPES AND STORIES FROM THE
CHEF BOYARDEE FAMILY

ANNA BOIARDI

AND STEPHANIE LYNESS

photographs by ELLEN SILVERMAN

STEWART, TABORI & CHANG   NEW YORK

Published in 2011 by Stewart, Tabori & Chang
An imprint of ABRAMS

All Chef Boyardee trademarks, packaging, and photographs are reprinted with permission from
ConAgra Foods, Omaha, Nebraska.

Library of Congress Cataloging-in-Publication Data
Boiardi, Anna.
Delicious Memories: recipes and stories from the
Chef Boyardee family / Anna Boiardi and Stephanie Lyness.
p. cm.
Includes index.
ISBN 978-1-58479-906-1 (alk. paper)
1. Cooking, Italian. 2. Brand name products—United States. I. Lyness,
Stephanie. II. Title.
TX723.B518 2011
641.5945—dc22
2010031269

Editor: Jennifer Levesque
Designer: Alissa Faden
Production Manager: Tina Cameron

The text of this book was composed in Sabon, Whitney, Commerce Gothic,
Engravers, and Sackers Gothic.

Printed in the U.S.A.
10 9 8 7 6 5 4 3 2

Stewart, Tabori & Chang books are available at special discounts when purchased in quantity for
premiums and promotions as well as fundraising or educational use. Special editions can also be
created to specification. For details, contact specialsales@abramsbooks.com or the address below.

ABRAMS
THE ART OF BOOKS SINCE 1949
115 West 18th Street
New York, NY 10011
www.abramsbooks.com

To my mother and father, for their endless
encouragement and support.

To my son, Jack IV.

And to my grandfather, Mario, and great uncles
Hector and Paul, who started the family traditions in
Piacenza and whose legacy continues to inspire me.

CONTENTS

TRADITION WITH A TWIST

FROM BOIARDI TO CHEF BOYARDEE

Fold and press. Then the other side: fold in toward the center, but this time, pinch. Back to the first side: fold to the center and pinch. And now it's like braiding—folding and pinching, back and forth from one side to the other, until the ricotta-spinach filling is entirely enclosed in the pasta. It looks like a tiny, braided loaf of challah. Well, mine looks like a tiny, slightly messy, braided loaf of challah.

I look over at the tray of tortelli that my mother has completed in about half the time it's taken me to put mine together. Each one neat and regular.

Nauseating.

To tell the truth, although I adore eating them, making tortelli is not really my thing. I'm more of a roast-chicken-with-rosemary, penne-with-broccoli, and asparagus-Parmesan kind of girl, the kind who prefers the simple, tasty, no-fuss recipes that I teach in my New York cooking classes. I want to be able to cook *something* for dinner out of my kitchen, every night, whether I've got five minutes or five hours. But these time-consuming little homemade stuffed pasta shapes my mother and I are making are a beloved specialty from my family's hometown in Italy. You won't find them anywhere outside of Piacenza (and here in my mother's New Jersey kitchen, of course). Even in Piacenza, where I ordered them in a restaurant last year, the chef had given up the traditional shape, cutting them into simple ravioli instead. They were a "more *contemporary* interpretation," the waiter explained when I complained. Right. The it-takes-way-too-long-to-make-them-the-traditional-way meaning of contemporary.

Not that I don't sympathize. Smearing a tiny spoonful of green-flecked filling on another square of pasta, I really do. Tortelli-making definitely belongs to another age, when life moved a lot slower and tortelli makers like me weren't distracted by telephones, computers, and BlackBerries. But since I got married and started cooking regularly for my husband, Jack, and myself, I've begun to recognize how important my family's values and culinary traditions have always been to me.

I got a shock a few years ago when my dad was ill and lost his memory for a brief period of time. During those few months, I suddenly faced the possibility that his memories could be lost to me forever. I realized how much I still had to discover about my family's history and traditions, traditions that are easy to forgo in fast-paced contemporary life, but which I want badly to pass along to my own kids someday. Cooking from my family's repertoire of traditional dishes is one way to inherit the family memories. So I keep on with the folding and pinching, hoping that by the time my kids are old enough to stand next to me in my kitchen making tortelli, I won't embarrass myself. And besides, it just makes me happy to be in the kitchen.

"Anna Maria! Are you watching the cake?"

She has eyes in the back of her head, my mother.

"Timer's on, Mom—it's under control."

We've got another Italian specialty in the oven, *pane degli angeli*. It's something like an angel food cake (and literally translates to "bread of angels"), made with beaten eggs, olive oil, and potato starch, baked in a springform pan. It's very, very local to the area where my mother grew up, and the recipe has been in our family forever. Unlike tortelli, it's a cinch to put together, and I make it all the time.

Another reason I'm determined to get these tortelli perfect is that I have a pretty spectacular culinary inheritance to live up to. From a very young age, I knew that my family made magic in the kitchen. If you've ever walked down the pasta aisle in a supermarket, you know my dad's family: The name is Boiardi . . . as in Chef Boyardee. They were restaurant people. Mario, my dad's father, and his brother, Hector, were chefs (as was their father). Hector and Mario founded the Chef Boyardee Company in 1928 with their elder brother, Paul. The three brothers pooled their resources to start the business (my dad likes to tell me how proud they were not to have to borrow any money at all). But Hector was really the driving force behind the brand. His is the cheerful face on the can, with mustache and chef's toque. You can see him in action on YouTube, selling one of his spaghetti dinners in a 1953 television commercial. "Give me fifteen minutes, and I'll give you a real Italian dinner!"

Chef Boiardi's, one of Uncle Hector's restaurants in Cleveland, Ohio.

"You can't write this story without historical context," my dad says. "Europe was old, social places were fixed. In those days, you had to leave home to find a job." America was growing rapidly at the beginning of the twentieth century. "New buildings were going up—new hotels, new restaurants—and they all required people to service them. The family wanted to find out what was over here."

The history of the brand is one of those only-in-America kinds of success stories. Paul came to New York in the early years of the century. He started out waiting tables at the Persian Room at the Plaza Hotel and worked his way up to the position of maître d'. "Hollywood good looks, and the manners of an English butler" my dad says of him—apparently a winning combination because by the 1930s, Paul was by far the best known and most influential maître d' in New York. At age seventeen, Hector followed Paul to New York. My grandfather came over a few years later; a resourceful fellow, he took a job as a waiter on the steamship and "forgot" to get back on when it left port. Anyway, Paul got both brothers work at the Plaza, Hector in the kitchen and my grandfather in the dining room. Mario, who was also a chef, could jump into the kitchen when they needed him.

Of the three brothers, I only knew Uncle Hector (we called him that, though he was really my great-uncle); my grandfather and Paul died before I was born. I remember Hector as a distinguished-looking man, always well

FROM LEFT TO RIGHT: Uncle Paul, Uncle Hector, my grandfather Mario, Carl Columbi (Secretary at Chef Boyardee); Milton, Pennsylvania.

dressed. A wonderful listener, patient with my childish questions, he would sit with me and tell stories like this one: During the Depression, a man came into Hector's restaurant, sat down, and ate dinner, then couldn't pay the bill. The waiter didn't want to make a scene, so he passed the problem on to his boss, who came out of the kitchen to talk to the guy.

"What happened?" Hector asked him.

"I was hungry," the man said.

"Don't sit down in the dining room and waste my waiters' time," Hector said. "Next time you're hungry, come to the kitchen and I'll feed you." He was sort of legendary in the family for his gentleness and that generous heart.

He was a whiz at mechanical stuff, too. He helped design several of the machines in the Chef Boyardee factory; in fact, a version of his meatball-making machine is still in use today. And my dad tells other stories about him. He was a real character: he loved to drive (generally over the speed limit), always with a cigar in his mouth. As a boy, my dad worked at the factory whenever he was out of school. He was crazy about Hector; his own father had died when my dad was in his twenties. He still gets a little choked up when he talks about Hector. "A working fool," he calls him.

The assembly line in the shipping room during the early days of the Chef Boyardee plant in Milton, Pennsylvania.

Like many European chefs of their generation, Hector and Mario started work very young; they began their training in the kitchen of the restaurant La Croce Bianca in Piacenza, peeling potatoes and taking out the garbage. Hector went on to apprentice in restaurants in Paris and London before arriving in the States. After the Plaza, when he was only nineteen or twenty, he was hired as the head chef at Barbetta, an Italian restaurant on Forty-sixth Street that recently celebrated its hundredth anniversary. When, at twenty-one, he was asked to run the kitchen at the Winton Hotel in Cleveland, he left his brothers in New York and moved west. He opened two more restaurants in Cleveland and worked at all of them at the same time. (Somehow he also managed to fit in Woodrow Wilson's wedding reception, which he catered at the Greenbrier Inn in West Virginia, in 1915.)

In 1924, he opened his own restaurant, Il Giardino d'Italia, serving the food he'd grown up with. His customers liked his tomato sauce so much that they started asking to take some home with them. Uncle Hector would fill glass milk bottles with the sauce, wrap up a little dried spaghetti and Parmesan cheese, and off they'd go. But when his customers kept bringing the bottles back for refills, he thought he'd better open up a place where he could make the sauce the main event, rather than just a sideline to the restaurant work.

So he put together a partnership with his brothers and took over a plant in Cleveland to can the sauce under the brand name Chef Boiardi Food Company. (Later on, when Americans had a hard time pronouncing the brand, they changed the name to spell it out phonetically: Chef Boyardee.) Mario came out to Cleveland with his wife and tiny son (my dad). They launched the company with three sauces: the tomato sauce everybody loved, a mushroom sauce, and a spicy Naples-style tomato sauce. "Three delightful flavors for a varied menu" was the slogan.

The business was an immediate success. By 1936, having outgrown the Cleveland facility, Hector and Mario moved the business to Milton, Pennsylvania—farm country—where tomatoes were plentiful. By then they'd expanded the line and were selling complete Italian dinners—clear cellophane packages combining a fistful of dried spaghetti, a can of sauce, and a can of grated Parmesan cheese.

Meanwhile, at the Plaza, Paul had gotten to be friendly with a man named John Hartford, the president of A&P supermarkets, by far the largest retailer of food in the United States at that time. One day, Paul said to John, "My brother has an operation that's canning Italian foods. Would A&P be interested in selling it?" John said, "Sure, go down and meet so-and-so." And that was that.

A&P took on the line, and then *everyone* took on the line. Business was so good that Paul left the Plaza to work full-time in Milton. During the thirties, Chef Boyardee was the top-selling Italian food product in supermarkets. The volume was *enormous*. Twenty thousand tons of tomatoes a season were converted to purée; the factory was the largest producer of mushrooms and the largest importer of Parmesan cheese and olive oil in the world. I think it's fair to say that those three men, with no formal education and very little money, can be credited with bringing Italian food to America.

The cake is out of the oven and cooling on a rack. My mother is reminiscing.

"Such a lot of work this used to be when I was young . . . and we really looked forward to eating it!"

My mother grew up in a radically different world. Dad was born in New York the year the Cleveland factory opened. By the time he left home for military school at thirteen, the family was well off and traveled regularly to Europe. (On Dad's first transatlantic ocean trip, he had dinner with a lovely blonde who turned out to be Grace Kelly—*that* was his world.) My mother grew up in a house at the end of a dirt road, without heat or indoor

Want something fast and filling and fun?

CHEF BOY-AR-DEE

Original advertisement for the "Spaghetti and Meat Balls" dinner.

plumbing. Meat was scarce. You didn't waste anything. Pane degli angeli was a once-a-year event, marking the end of the grape harvest. The women of the town would gather at the bakery to make the cakes because the baker's was the only oven in town.

My parents didn't meet until Dad was visiting his family in Piacenza in the sixties, but that's another story (it's on page 92). My mom's a Sophia Loren type: beautiful, sexy, and dramatic. Also hard working, a genius of a cook, strict (with me), a little quirky, and incredibly practical, as I imagine all the women in her family had to be.

She's always been a stickler for doing things *right*. "You have to know the right way," she'd tell me. "Certain steps are necessary. It's important to take time, and to have pride. Not everything has to be so fast and simple." She drummed into me the value of careful attention to detail. She taught respect for all the work that goes into cooking and feeding people, from washing dishes, to stirring custard the correct way (clockwise), to wrapping pans of lasagne to give as Christmas presents and tying the holiday candles in velvet ribbon. Sometimes her perfectionism drove me crazy! But when I hear people talk about the drudgery of cooking and maintaining a household, I'm glad for her perspective. Cooking is well respected in Italy anyway, but she made domestic work seem like an art.

With the last of the tortelli folded, pinched, pressed, and cajoled into shape, we set aside enough for tonight's dinner, then wrap and freeze the rest.

I love having grown up with such a strong sense of family history and kitchen tradition. It's given me a sense of home that seems particularly important these days. As we get more global and young people don't cook so much, traditions are more and more likely to be lost. I believe in making tortelli the "right" way (otherwise, they're just ravioli, aren't they?).

But I also believe in experimentation and adaptation. (If high school chemistry hadn't been such a bear, I tell my dad, I probably would've liked to be a scientist; he reminds me of the afternoons I stayed late at school, chem lab goggles affixed to my head, blowing up—literally!—lab experiments, as I tried to get them right.) My grandfather and his brothers successfully adapted traditional recipes to the technology of canning and mass production. My grandmother didn't have refrigeration, but I do. And I have access to so many more ingredients than my mother did when she was my age; they make cooking more efficient, and I take advantage of them. I buy good quality *grated* Parmesan and pecorino cheeses. I'll use ready-made dough from the market around the corner, and sometimes I'll jazz up a can of Hunt's tomato sauce for pizza. I sometimes substitute sliced American cheese for Fontina, and I'm quite happy with Uncle Ben's converted rice (follow the cooking instructions on the box).

It's important to experiment with what works for you; perfectionism

Quick, easy, and inexpensive were important selling points then, and remain true today.

The first line of Chef Boyardee products.

should never, ever get in the way of being able to put together a good meal in whatever time you've got to cook it. I think of it as tradition with a twist. The twist often means convenience. But not always. Sometimes I "twist" a recipe to appeal to my taste; sometimes, because I need to use what I have in the refrigerator. My mother hardly ever makes a recipe the same way twice! Recipes can and should evolve—they always have. I just try to hold on to what made them special in the first place.

Good food doesn't have to be fancy or complicated, either. I adore giving dinner parties, and I've been surprised to find that the simplest foods are almost always the most sought after. I'm cooking for a sophisticated bunch; they eat out regularly at very good restaurants. And they line up for these incredibly down-to-earth dishes from my family's repertoire: green beans with red wine vinegar and chopped parsley, heirloom tomato salad, frittata with onion and zucchini, potato salad with garlic and parsley, turkey meatballs. Freshly made, home-cooked food has an appeal that transcends fanciness.

One of the things I emphasize in my classes is that it really is possible to make time for cooking—necessary, in fact, given the crazy lives we all lead. My twenty-first-century life is much more complicated than my mother's. I can't get home for dinner every night, and I often don't have much time to cook. But I've figured out how to organize things so there's always something to eat in the house. My husband and I eat much more simply than my parents, who will start with the tortelli as a first course, move on to an entrée and vegetable, and perhaps even have dessert. Too much work for me! Unless I'm cooking for a special occasion, I serve pasta as the entrée. When I get home tonight, the tortelli will go into a pot of boiling water while I make a salad. I'll sauce the pasta with melted butter and sage, and presto! It's dinner.

Even without a tortelli-making mother at your side, if you've got a few things on hand, it's quite possible to boil linguine, cook a tomato sauce, and have a nice homemade dish in under an hour. Penne with broccoli is even easier; that's the recipe I give my friends who call from the produce aisle of the supermarket at five P.M. to ask me what to cook for dinner that night. In Italy, life moves slowly, and we spend much of the day thinking about food—talking about food, shopping for food, eating food. It's different in America, where we schedule more tightly. I make it easy on myself. For everyday cooking, I rely on a strategically stocked pantry, a weekly date (Sunday) with the supermarket, and a handful of quick-and-doable recipes. On pages 18–19 you'll find my pared-down pantry list: 12 things to keep on hand in your pantry and fridge (plus spices) and 12 cooking utensils so that you can *always* put together a homemade meal, with little or no shopping.

But the classes I teach also underline the importance of maintaining some traditions around eating even if you're dining very informally; I am my mother's daughter, after all.

The Boiardis have always kept a tradition of Sunday family dinners. Hector closed his restaurants on Sundays to cook for the family, and I grew up with a big, Sunday family meal. Jack and I are less ambitious, but we make sure to have Sunday evenings to ourselves, even if we just go out for pizza. In the winter, I cook the yummy polenta pasticciata—polenta baked with tomato, cheese, and mushrooms—that I used to make with my Nonna Anna. While we cooked, she often told the story of how her own mother, faced with the responsibility of feeding a child, brought the two of them to New York with just the salamis she'd stuffed into her pockets for the trip.

Always Nonna Anna ended the story with "See, Anna? Food is so important. You must be grateful for food and tradition." My children will never know Nonna Anna, but they will know her polenta. And when I cook it, I think of her and her pockets, heavy with salamis, and it makes me smile.

It sometimes seems as if all my childhood memories are tied to cooking and eating. Food remains a comfortable and dependable constant. It's also a little bit magical. . . . It was food that changed Boiardi history. This cookbook pays tribute to all the wonderful meals that the Boiardis have created and shared as a family, both in Italy and the United States. The recipes hold all stories—of our Italy, and of our America.

Making a home is about cooking good food. You can stick with the food you grew up with, use my recipes, or borrow someone else's traditions. My hope is that these recipes will encourage readers who do know how to cook to do so more regularly and those who don't yet to learn. Every family has traditions. Cooking is a way to live them.

12 ESSENTIALS TO MAKE 15 DINNERS

Many cookbooks give you a list of food items and cooking tools you need to set up your kitchen. I want to do something simpler. There are some pieces of kitchen equipment that, sometime in your life, you should acquire. But I don't want people *not* to make things just because they don't have all the right tools. An aluminum pan works really, really well until such time as someone gives you an actual roasting pan. Or maybe your kitchen, like most New York kitchens, just isn't big enough, won't *ever* be big enough, to store a roasting pan.

So I recommend that you start small, like my grandfather did. Here's a collection of rock-bottom, must-have cooking tools and a pared-down grocery list, so that you always have the basics to put together at least fifteen different recipes, with salad, for dinner.

Many recipes in the book also include a sidebar called "Kitchen Stuff," listing other useful cooking tools and serving pieces, so that when the time comes to outfit your kitchen more comprehensively, you'll know what to look for.

12 THINGS TO KEEP ON HAND...

IN YOUR PANTRY	IN YOUR FRIDGE AND FREEZER	IN YOUR KITCHEN CUPBOARD	IN YOUR SPICE RACK
Dried pasta (penne, spaghetti, rigatoni, linguine, bucatini)	Finely grated Parmesan cheese	Box grater	Salt
Assorted cans (35, 28, and 14 ounces) plum tomatoes (preferably San Marzano) in juice	Finely grated pecorino cheese	Colander	Black pepper
Extra-virgin olive oil	Large eggs	Large skillet	Peperoncino (red pepper flakes)
Wine vinegar (red or white)	Pinot Grigio wine	Large pot	Garlic powder
Garlic	Lettuce	Medium saucepan	Worcestershire sauce
Onions (I like sweet Vidalia onions)	Fresh basil	Wooden spoon	Dried oregano
All-purpose flour	Fresh Italian parsley	Chef's knife	Whole nutmeg
Dried bread crumbs	Lemons	Food mill	Dried rosemary
Polenta	Unsalted butter	Ladle, preferably a large one	
Canned low-sodium chicken broth	Dried porcini mushrooms	Cutting board	
Nonpareil capers	Ketchup	9-by-13-inch baking dish	
Arborio or carnaroli rice	Fresh plum tomatoes	Baking sheet	

TO MAKE THESE 15 DELIGHTFUL DINNERS —WITH SALAD

(HALF OF THEM REQUIRE A QUICK RUN TO THE MARKET FOR A FEW EXTRAS)

80
*Uncle Hector's Tagliatelle with Tomato Sauce
"Il Giardino"*

89
Spaghetti Aglio e Olio

84
Penne with Mushroom Sauce

35
My Favorite Frittata
(plus milk)

47
Risotto with Parmesan Cheese

51
Risotto with Porcini Mushrooms

83
*Southern Italian Style Rigatoni
with Roasted Tomatoes*

74
Leaving-Home Penne Rigate with Broccoli
(plus broccoli)

90
Bucatini Amatriciana
(plus bacon)

49
Risotto with Asparagus
(plus asparagus)

140
Nonna Anna's Well-Patted Meat Loaf
(plus meat loaf mix)

127
*Chicken Cutlets with Ham, Cheese, Tomatoes,
and Capers*
(plus chicken, ham, and Fontina)

116
Jack's Turkey Meatballs in Tomato Sauce
(plus ground turkey)

132
Nonna Anna's Polenta Pasticciata
(plus Fontina)

68
Pizza Margherita
(plus mozzarella cheese and pizza dough)

FIRST BITES: ANTIPASTI

In Italy, our meals always start off with an antipasto, which just means something to nibble on while everyone has a glass of wine and socializes. When we're eating out in a restaurant in Italy, we order several antipasti for the center of the table, and everyone shares. They're not just for more formal occasions, though. It's a nice way to make people feel taken care of. My mom makes sure there are a few antipasti on her kitchen counter when Jack and I come by for dinner. She presses cocktail plates into our hands, and we snack on olives, little toasts called bruschetta, and plates of grilled vegetables and roasted peppers while we talk about the day. It makes things feel special.

Sadly, neither I, nor my students, have a lot of time for this ritual in our everyday lives, so we need recipes that can be put together quickly. The first two recipes—Antipasto di Salumi, and Tuna, Anchovies, Olives, and Artichokes—require no cooking at all, and a third, Grape Tomato Bruschetta, just needs some bread-toasting.

An antipasto or two can keep you feeling organized if you're running late. Worst-case scenario? Your dinner friends show up just as you walk in the door, shopping bags in hand. You assemble one of the antipasti while your friends are taking their coats off. Get someone to open a bottle of wine, and voilà! Everybody's taken care of for a while. Enough time for you to make dinner.

Antipasti *do* come in very handy for dinner parties because they can be made ahead and served at room temperature: I set out two, three, or even four of them on the table for my guests to snack on as they arrive. They also make wonderful cocktail party food arranged on top of bruschetta, because people can pop them easily into their mouths between conversations. Some recipes—the roasted peppers, grilled vegetables, potato salad, and caponata—can double as dinner vegetables.

This is a short list of my favorite antipasti, combining the most delicious, doable, and traditional recipes that I grew up with.

ANTIPASTO DI SALUMI

SERVES 4

½ POUND	olives	
¼ POUND	spicy salami, thinly sliced	
¼ POUND	sweet salami or coppa, thinly sliced	
¼ POUND	prosciutto cotto (cooked ham), thinly sliced	
¼ POUND	prosciutto, very thinly sliced	
¼ POUND	mortadella, thinly sliced	
	Breadsticks	
	Sliced baguette or bruschetta crackers	
	KITCHEN STUFF	
	A really pretty oval serving platter	

SHOPPING WITH ANNA

There's no magic to the selection of meats; variety is what counts. You could forgo one of the meats and substitute ¼-pound cubed Parmesan cheese. Good-quality, store-bought marinated vegetables (artichoke hearts are traditional) can replace olives. Or serve the vegetables in addition. We generally serve a raw ham (prosciutto) and a cooked ham (prosciutto cotto); hams sold as "French ham" are most like the prosciutto cotto we eat in Italy.

The area around Piacenza is known for its locally made pork salumi—which means cured meats—such as prosciutto, capicollo (which we call coppa in Piacenza), pancetta, salame, and cacciatorini. When my mom was growing up, a single pig slaughtered in the fall would feed the family for an entire year. How much of the animal can you eat?? (Stop. I don't really want to know.)

Before it was legal to import salumi into the States, my grandmother used to smuggle it through customs sewn into the hem of her skirts. (My mom went one better: she had a false-bottomed suitcase custom made to sneak hunks of Parmesan and salumi into the country.) My grandmother's short, round frame hid the meats pretty well, but as an added measure of security, my brother and I were delegated to be her "beards" when we traveled with her.

"Act like you're really tired," she would prompt us as we approached the customs officers. Wanting to spare an overburdened old lady with jet-lagged kids, they quickly shooed us through.

These days you can find cured meats at a good Italian deli or even in the supermarket. The idea here is to cater to a variety of tastes. I like sweeter meats, for instance, while Jack likes them spicy (like our personalities, I tell him), so I always buy one sweet and one spicy salami to serve along with the hams. Ask the person behind the deli counter to slice the meats very thin. The five meats listed in the recipe are just suggestions to get you going. You can serve more or fewer varieties, or add cheese. It's your party.

PLACE THE OLIVES in a small, pretty bowl in the center of a large, decorative platter. Arrange each variety of meat separately around the olives: the salami and coppa can be laid out in overlapping rows. Drape the prosciutto slices, one next to the other. Do the same with the cooked ham. Fold the mortadella slices in half and then in half again to make triangles, and overlap them, one next to the other. Pay attention to color as you're arranging; the lighter-colored mortadella and cooked ham will make the darker-colored meats pop.

Put the breadsticks and crackers or bread in a basket. Set a stack of small plates alongside the antipasto arrangement.

ROASTED RED, YELLOW, AND ORANGE PEPPERS

SERVES 4

I almost always include this recipe in a class for beginning cooks. Everyone has eaten roasted peppers—at a restaurant, or from a deli, or a jar. People just assume they're hard to make. And discovering that they're not takes some of the fear out of cooking right away. At the end of the class, everyone is filled with pride to have mastered this difficult thing the first time out.

These peppers make a nice antipasto on their own, as one element of a more varied platter, or as a topping for bruschetta. They also add great color and flavor to other dishes: a plate of grilled vegetables (page 26), a plain turkey sandwich, or a tomato-mozzarella salad (see sidebar page 31). If you have a panini maker at home (one of my favorite kitchen tools), mozzarella and roasted peppers make *great* panini. These peppers will last for days in the refrigerator. Homemade roasted peppers are so much better than anything you can buy in jar—they are definitely worth a try!

PREHEAT THE BROILER to high and arrange an oven rack 4 to 6 inches from the element.

Wipe the peppers clean with a paper towel (do not wash). Cut off and discard the tops and stems. Cut each pepper in half through the stem ends, and pull out the seeds with your fingers. Cut out the white ribs with a small knife.

Place the pepper halves, skin side up, in a shallow foil pan or baking sheet. Broil until the skins are blackened, about 15 minutes. Remove the pan from the oven, cover with foil, and let cool for 1 hour.

Peel the skins off the cooled peppers with your fingers. Cut the peppers into 1-inch strips (see sidebar) and place them in a bowl. Sprinkle with the salt and pepper. Add the olive oil, garlic, and, if you're using them, the capers. Toss to coat the peppers with the seasonings. Set aside at room temperature until you're ready to serve, or cover and refrigerate for up to 3 days; bring the peppers to room temperature before serving.

1	*firm red bell pepper*
1	*firm yellow bell pepper*
1	*firm orange bell pepper*
¾ TEASPOON	*salt*
PINCH	*freshly ground pepper*
⅓ CUP	*extra-virgin olive oil*
1 CLOVE	*garlic, cut into thin slivers*
1 TABLESPOON	*nonpareil capers (the tiny ones) in vinegar, drained (optional)*

TUNA, ANCHOVIES, OLIVES, AND ARTICHOKES

SERVES 6

Here's another super-easy antipasto that generations of Italian families have made in generations of kitchens. When my mom was growing up, canned tuna came in large, beautiful chunks, packed into foot-high cans and covered in olive oil. (When she talks about it, her eyes light up and she gestures a lot, so I believe that it tasted really *fabulous*.) It was sold by the pound at the local grocery store. She would tell the owner how much she wanted, he would ladle it into a jar for her, and she'd take it home, maybe to make into this antipasto.

One of the great things about this recipe is that it's just a collection of store-bought foods that—with the exception of the lettuce—you can keep in the pantry. If I've got sliced salami, I set out a dish of that, too, and add a plate of sliced bread.

Anchovies, while traditional (and very high in calcium), are not my favorite food. (Except on pizza. When I'm in the mood for something salty. Anchovies add just that little *kick*. . . .) If you or your guests aren't fans either, replace the anchovies with chunks of Parmesan cheese.

4 LARGE LEAVES	*Boston lettuce, washed and spun dry*
1 (7-OUNCE) JAR	*Italian, oil-packed tuna*
⅔ POUND	*green and black Cerignola olives, drained*
1 (3-OUNCE) JAR	*Italian, oil-packed anchovies (optional)*
⅔ POUND	*marinated artichoke hearts*
	Breadsticks, for serving

COVER A LARGE, DECORATIVE PLATTER with the lettuce leaves. Spoon the tuna onto one leaf. Mound the olives on another. Spoon the anchovies on a third leaf, and the artichoke hearts on the fourth (they'll overflow a bit onto the platter). Put the breadsticks into a tall, decorative glass. Voilà!

THE TWIST

The best tuna for this dish is a good Italian brand packed in olive oil. If you can't find one, drain a can of oil- or water-packed tuna, put it in a bowl, and pour in enough olive oil to cover it generously. Let it sit overnight or a couple of days in the refrigerator so that it picks up the flavor of the oil.

GRILLED PARTY VEGETABLES

2	*firm Italian eggplants*
3	*firm zucchini*
	Salt
	Olive oil spray, for grilling
5 TABLESPOONS	*extra-virgin olive oil*
2 CLOVES	*garlic, sliced*
	Freshly ground pepper
2 NICE SPRIGS	*fresh basil for garnish*
	KITCHEN STUFF
	A grill pan (preferably nonstick)

SHOPPING WITH ANNA
I buy the smaller eggplants, called "Italian" eggplants, because they have fewer seeds than the large guys and they're less watery.

These vegetables are actually better if you make them a day ahead, which means they're ideal for parties: The vegetables get a chance to absorb the taste of the garlic, and you get a chance to get a dish out of the way! I usually put them with something else—I'll set out a plate of sliced meats, say, or tuck thick ribbons of roasted peppers (page 23) between the zucchini and eggplant (the peppers are great for color). And I make extra if I can afford the time, because I like having them around the house. They're an easy side dish for dinner, and, with a couple of slices of mozzarella cheese, they're wonderful on panini.

Eggplant and zucchini are both watery vegetables. Salting them for several hours before cooking them pulls out some of the liquid (and putting a weight on top helps press out more); it makes them much tastier! And this recipe doubles, triples, quadruples—however many people you're feeding—very successfully; just use two colanders, one for each vegetable.

TRIM OFF THE ENDS and cut the eggplants crosswise into rounds about ⅓ inch thick. Trim off the ends and cut the zucchini lengthwise into ⅓-inch-thick strips; cut the zucchini strips crosswise into four equal rectangles, each about 3 inches long.

Set a colander on top of a deep plate. Put the eggplant slices into the colander, sprinkle with 1 teaspoon salt and toss with a fork so that each slice is seasoned with some of the salt. Add the zucchini to the colander, sprinkle with another 1 teaspoon of salt, and toss with the zucchini. (Be careful to keep zucchini and eggplant relatively separate from each other; the eggplant gives off a bitter liquid, and you want that on the plate, not dripping onto your zucchini.) Set a plate directly on top of the zucchini and put something heavy on top (I use a 28-ounce can of tomatoes) to help press out the water. Let stand at least 1 hour (3 hours is even better).

Spread a paper towel on your work surface. Remove the vegetable slices from the colander and arrange them in a single layer on the paper towel; cover them with a second paper towel and blot well so that the vegetables are good and dry. Remove the vegetables to a baking dish. Continue blotting this way, changing paper towels as they get wet, until all the vegetables are dry.

Heat a grill pan (preferably nonstick) on the stove over medium-high heat until hot, 3 to 5 minutes. Spray the pan lightly with olive-oil spray. Arrange a single layer of vegetable slices on the grill. Cook until you see nice grill marks on one side, 2 to 4 minutes. (If it takes longer than that, you probably need to raise the heat under the pan.) Turn, and cook until the other side is marked and the vegetables are soft, 2 to 4 more minutes. Remove to a large platter. Continue until all the vegetables are cooked.

Drizzle the vegetables with the oil, turning them with a fork so that all the pieces are coated and very moist. (The vegetables will absorb a lot of oil, so if they seem dry, don't hesitate to add another tablespoon or 2.) Scatter the garlic slices on top. Sprinkle with pepper. Set aside for at least 2 hours. Or refrigerate, covered, overnight; bring to room temperature before serving.

To serve, shingle the eggplant on one half of a serving platter, the zucchini on the other. Decorate with the basil.

THE TWIST

Unlike my grandparents and their grandparents, who didn't have access to such things, I find it very convenient to use those aluminum pans you buy in the supermarket for a number of purposes. They come in a million different sizes. They're great for stashing ingredients as you prepare them. They're perfect of potlucks. They're lightweight. They're washable and/or disposable. And if you find yourself cooking for twenty, let alone eighty, they're indispensable.

CAPONATA, MY WAY

SERVES 8 TO 10

4	*firm Italian eggplants, about 1½ pounds total*
4	*firm zucchini*
	Salt
5	*large plum tomatoes, or 1 (14-ounce) can Italian plum tomatoes, with juice*
2	*firm red bell peppers*
2	*firm yellow bell peppers*
1 CUP	*extra-virgin olive oil*
2 CLOVES	*garlic, chopped*
2 TABLESPOONS	*chopped fresh Italian parsley*
2	*medium onions, roughly chopped*
	Freshly ground black pepper or peperoncino (red pepper flakes)

SHOPPING WITH ANNA

When you're buying zucchini, steer clear of the really gigantic ones. They have mushy, seed-filled interiors. Look for medium-sized vegetables that weigh 4 to 6 ounces each.

Caponata is a vegetable dish that's made all over Italy. Everybody has a slightly different recipe, but the version most recognizable to Americans is Sicilian, typically made with olives and capers, as well as vinegar and sugar to give it the familiar sweet-and-sour taste. Our version is made with nothing more than vegetables, seasoning, and olive oil, with the vegetables all cooked together in a big pan on top of the stove.

This recipe is bicultural, the result of a year I spent at school in the south of France when I was twenty. The lady of the house where I stayed was a wonderful cook, and she often made ratatouille, a vegetable stew that is similar to caponata—at least the way we make it in Piacenza (not surprising—southern France is not far from northern Italy). But instead of cooking everything all together, Madame Gueno cooked the vegetables one at a time and then combined them at the end.

Madame's method appealed to me because it considers each vegetable's cooking time (peppers take longer than zucchini, for instance). Nothing overcooks, I can taste each vegetable, and nothing turns to mush. I imported it to my mother's kitchen when I returned from France. The final step—number 9—is my own. Baking gently melds the flavors.

You can serve this as an appetizer or vegetable side dish, but I make it more often as an antipasto. When it's spooned on top of toasted bread slices or bruschetta crackers, people love it. Jack, in particular, is crazy for it. (He begs me to make it every year for his birthday, a big bash with about seventy to a hundred guests . . . and how can I say no?)

If you do plan to serve it with bruschetta, cut the vegetables very small—about ¼-inch dice. I make it in large quantities because it's more than a little chopping (which I don't want to do too often). It's good cold or hot, and it gets better as it sits—two days after you make it, it's perfect.

SET YOURSELF UP with two colanders. Trim the stems from the eggplant. Slice the eggplant lengthwise ⅓ to ½ inch thick. Cut the slices lengthwise into strips about ⅓ to ½ inch wide, and cut those strips crosswise into cubes. Put the eggplant cubes into one of the colanders. Cube the zucchini the same way, and put it into the second colander. Thoroughly toss each vegetable with about 2 teaspoons salt. Set a plate directly on top of the vegetables in each colander, and weight the plates with a couple of large cans. (This will press out the water

and intensify the flavor of the vegetables.) Put the colanders in the sink, or on two deep plates to catch the water, and set them aside for at least 2 hours to drain.

If you're using fresh tomatoes, bring a saucepan of water to a boil over medium-high heat. Set a plate near the stove. Add the tomatoes to the water and let them bob around until the skin begins to pull away from the flesh, 1 to 2 minutes. Remove the tomatoes to the plate with a slotted spoon or "spider" and let them cool a few minutes. When they're cool enough to handle, peel off the skins with your fingers. Chop the tomatoes, put them in a bowl, and set them aside. (If you're using canned tomatoes, coarsely chop the tomatoes—a food processor works just fine for this—and set them aside in a bowl with their juice.)

Cut off and discard the tops of the bell peppers. Cut the peppers in half through the stem ends and pull out the seeds with your fingers. Carefully cut out the fleshy, white ribs with a small knife. Then slice the peppers into strips ⅓ to ½ inch wide; cut the strips crosswise into squares.

Dump the eggplant out onto paper toweling. Cover with more paper toweling and pat dry completely. Do the same with the zucchini, keeping the vegetables separate.

Set a 9-by-13-inch baking dish next to the stove. Place two large skillets on top of two burners over medium heat. Add ¼ cup oil to each pan and heat until the oil is hot enough to sizzle when you add a piece of eggplant. Then put the egg-plant into one pan and the zucchini into the other. Cook, stirring every now and then with a wooden spoon, until the vegetables just begin to color, about 20 minutes. Scrape all the vegetables out into the baking dish.

Turn the heat to low under one skillet. Add another ¼ cup oil and the garlic to the skillet. Heat the oil until you smell the garlic a bit, 1 to 2 minutes. (Don't let the garlic color or it will get strong tasting.) Now add the chopped tomato (fresh or canned, with juices), ¼ teaspoon salt, and the parsley. Cover and sim-mer very gently until the tomatoes are soft and saucy, about 25 minutes for fresh or 35 minutes for canned. Scrape into the baking dish.

While the tomatoes cook, add the remaining ¼ cup oil to the second pan, set it over medium heat, and heat until a little piece of onion sizzles when you add it to the pan. Add the chopped onion and cook 5 minutes. Add the diced peppers and 1½ teaspoons salt. Cook, stirring now and then, until the peppers are very soft, about 25 more minutes. Add to the baking dish.

Preheat the oven to 350°F and center a rack in the oven.

Add ⅛ teaspoon black pepper or peperoncino to the vegetables in the baking dish and gently stir all the vegetables together. Taste, and add salt or pepper to your liking. (We don't really do spicy, but you can add more red pepper, if you like.) Cover the baking dish with aluminum foil and bake 25 minutes.

PARTY PEPPERS

I slice roasted peppers thick or thin, depending on my plans for them. A 1-inch width is fine for a salad, as part of an antipasto platter, for a sandwich or panini, or with grilled vegetables.

For parties, I like to cut them very fine and mound them on top of bruschetta. I also use them to decorate tomato-mozzarella salads: Slice ripe tomatoes 1 inch thick. Stack a 1-inch-thick round of fresh mozzarella on top of each tomato slice. Drape one thinly sliced ribbon of red, and one thinly sliced ribbon of yellow pepper in the center of the cheese. Arrange on a big, white platter.

GRAPE TOMATO BRUSCHETTA

SERVES 4

These are like open-faced tomato sandwiches—toasted bread topped with mini grape tomato and basil salads. Bruschetta comes from verb *bruscare*, which means "to toast over coals." Bruschetta are great for parties. If people are arriving at seven, I make the tomato topping in the afternoon, and let it sit at room temperature. I'll start toasting the bread at six thirty, top the toasts with the tomatoes, and put the bruschetta out on a platter. When people arrive, the bruschetta are still a little warm, the toast hasn't gotten soggy yet, and the house smells wonderful!

I make bruschetta with baguettes or ciabatta bread, but you can use any bread you like. If you use baguette, cut the bread on the diagonal into 1½-inch-thick slices and toast it just like the ciabatta.

The basil is cut into thin strips, called a "chiffonade." Stack the leaves, roll them like a cigar, and cut them crosswise as thinly as you can.

IN A MIXING BOWL, combine the quartered tomatoes, onion, basil, olive oil, salt, and pepper. Mix gently. Taste for seasoning and add more salt, if you think it needs it. Set aside at room temperature. (Do not refrigerate—you'll lose the taste of the tomato. They'll be fine at room temperature for up to 2 hours.)

Cut the ciabatta lengthwise into four 1-inch-thick pieces. Halve each piece crosswise.

Preheat the broiler and arrange an oven rack 4 to 6 inches from the element. Arrange the bread slices on a baking sheet and toast until golden brown; turn the slices and toast the other side.

While the toast is still warm, rub one side of each slice with the cut side of a half garlic clove—the garlic will melt into the toast.

Using a pastry brush, brush the same side of each piece of toast with olive oil.

With a slotted spoon, spoon some of the tomato mixture on top, leaving the juices in the bowl (they'll just make the toast soggy). Arrange the bruschetta on a platter and serve them within half an hour.

1 (10-OUNCE) BASKET	*ripe grape tomatoes, quartered*
1½ TABLESPOONS	*finely chopped red onion*
2 TABLESPOONS	*thinly sliced fresh basil*
½ CUP	*extra-virgin olive oil, plus about 2 tablespoons for brushing the toast*
½ TEASPOON	*salt, or as needed*
¼ TEASPOON	*freshly ground pepper*
½	*ciabatta loaf*
3 CLOVES	*garlic, peeled and halved*
KITCHEN STUFF	
	A good serrated bread knife
	Pastry brush

MY FAVORITE FRITTATA

SERVES 4

Frittatas, which are something like omelets only easier to make (no folding), can, like omelets, be made with lots of different ingredients. This is my favorite combination. Frittatas are traditionally served as an antipasto. But they taste much too good to be relegated to a part of the meal that I mostly don't have time to make. So I often serve this for a weekday dinner with a salad.

A frittata also makes fabulous cocktail food: once it's cooked, I cut it into little circles with a 2-inch round cookie cutter, then use a bit of mayonnaise to paste the rounds on toasted French bread slices or store-bought bruschetta crackers. They go like hotcakes.

You can make this in any skillet from 9 inches to 12 inches across. Just make sure it's nonstick and ovenproof. A 9-inch frittata will take a bit longer to cook because it's thicker.

CRACK THE EGGS into a bowl. Add the milk, grated cheeses, herbs, and ¼ teaspoon each salt and pepper. Beat the mixture with a fork to break up the eggs and blend the ingredients. Set aside.

In a 9- to 12-inch nonstick skillet, heat the oil over medium-low heat. Test the oil with a slice of onion; when it sizzles, the oil is ready. Add the onion and cook until it's soft and translucent, 8 to 10 minutes. (Do not allow the onion to brown! If begins to go golden, turn the heat down.) If you're using zucchini, add it 5 minutes into the cooking and cook until both onion and zucchini are nice and soft, 5 to 7 more minutes.

Turn the heat to low. Pour the egg mixture into the pan and let it cook until the edges have set but the middle is still wobbly, about 10 minutes (for a 10-inch skillet).

Heat the broiler and arrange an oven rack about 4 inches from the element. Wrap the handle of the skillet in aluminum foil to protect it from the heat. Place the skillet under the broiler and broil until the top turns golden brown, 2 to 4 minutes, depending on your broiler. Remove the pan from the oven and let the frittata cool for a few minutes. Loosen it from the pan with a spatula and slide it out onto a serving plate. Cut into wedges.

8	*large eggs*
2 TABLESPOONS	*milk*
¼ CUP	*finely grated Parmesan cheese*
¼ CUP	*finely grated pecorino cheese*
2 TABLESPOONS	*chopped fresh Italian parsley*
2 TABLESPOONS	*chopped fresh basil*
	Salt and freshly ground pepper
3 TABLESPOONS	*extra-virgin olive oil*
1	*small Vidalia (or other sweet) onion, finely sliced*
1	*medium zucchini, trimmed, and sliced into thin rounds (optional)*

POTATO SALAD
ITALIAN STYLE

SERVES 4

2½ POUNDS	*little red potatoes, unpeeled but washed*
I CUP	*extra-virgin olive oil*
½	*carrot, very finely chopped*
I CLOVE	*garlic, minced*
2 TABLESPOONS	*chopped fresh Italian parsley*
2 TABLESPOONS	*red wine vinegar*
I TEASPOON	*salt*
¼ TEASPOON	*freshly ground pepper*

This is what potato salad tastes like, Italian style. I make it for summer barbecues. It's no harder to put together than the American version, but it gets people's attention because it's a little different and very good. If you're like me and don't really love mayonnaise (it's not an Italian thing), this is a good alternative.

Last summer, Jack and I were invited to a friend's house in the Hamptons for the afternoon and dinner. We arrived thinking it would be just the four of us, and I figured I'd help with dinner because I'm the only one of the crowd who cooks. But throughout the afternoon, the guest list slowly grew to about ten as friends dropped by, saying, "Oh, are *you* making dinner? We'll stay!"

Well, what could I say? I improvised. We grilled steaks and peppers, and I made one large vat of potato salad and another of green salad. Everyone was happy.

You dress the potatoes while they're still warm, because they absorb the oil and flavorings better that way. Chopped up carrot adds a little crunch, and its bright color is pretty with the green of the parsley. This is a very practical recipe: make and eat it one day, refrigerate the leftovers, and use it the next day in a Niçoise salad (page 170).

PUT A COLANDER in the sink. Put the potatoes in a saucepan and add cold water to cover by about 1 inch. Bring the water to a boil, reduce the heat, and simmer until the tip of a small knife slides easily into the potatoes, 15 to 20 minutes. Drain in the colander.

When the potatoes are cool enough to handle, halve or quarter them, depending on their size, and place them in a large bowl. Add the oil and stir gently so that the potatoes are entirely coated (they will absorb a lot of oil). Add the carrot, garlic, parsley, vinegar, salt, and pepper, and mix well. Serve warm, or at room temperature.

CHRISTMAS EVE BACCALÀ

SERVES 6 TO 8

Salt cod, or baccalà, in Italian, has been a Boiardi family tradition for Christmas Eve for far longer than I can remember, and no Boiardi family cookbook would be complete without it. Salt cod is a traditional—and, literally, centuries-old—ingredient in Italy. (I'm beginning to run into it on restaurant menus in New York City, too.) Earlier generations of Boiardis would have eaten it at their meatless Christmas Eve dinners, along with marinated eel and maybe a meatless gnocchi.

Unlike fresh cod, salt cod has a sturdy texture that stands up well to this vinegar marinade. The cod is soaked for two days to remove all the salt and rehydrate the fish. Then it's floured, sautéed, and marinated for up to several days.

PUT THE COD into a bowl and add cold water to cover. Refrigerate 48 hours, changing the water every 12 hours. Drain and pat dry on paper towels.

For the marinade, heat the olive oil in a saucepan over medium heat. Add the onion rings and cook until softened, about 7 minutes. Add the carrot and celery and cook until all the vegetables are very soft, 5 to 6 more minutes. Sprinkle with salt and pepper, add the bay leaves and vinegar. Stir well, reduce the heat, and simmer, uncovered, for 20 minutes. Remove from the heat and let cool completely.

Line a baking dish or a large plate with paper towels. Put the flour on a plate. Dredge the cod in the flour and pat off the excess; place on a large plate or baking sheet. Heat the vegetable oil in a frying pan over medium heat until the oil smokes. Add as many pieces of cod to the pan as will fit and cook on both sides until golden brown, 10 to 15 minutes total. Transfer them to the paper-towel-lined baking dish to drain. Cook the remaining pieces of cod and drain. Let cool completely.

Arrange the cooled cod in a baking dish large enough to hold it in a single layer. Pour the cooled marinade over. Cover and refrigerate at least overnight or up to 3 days.

2 POUNDS	salt cod, cut into 2½-by-3-inch pieces
½ CUP	olive oil
1	large onion, sliced into very thin rings
1	small carrot, very finely chopped
3 STALKS	celery, bumpy side peeled with a vegetable peeler, very finely chopped
5	medium bay leaves
1¼ CUPS	white vinegar
	Salt and freshly ground pepper
1 CUP	all-purpose flour
1 CUP	vegetable oil

37

SOUPS, RISOTTI, AND OTHER PRIMI

In a traditional, multicourse Italian meal, the *primi* (which means "firsts") come between the antipasto and the entrée. A primo might be a soup, a small plate of pasta, gnocchi, polenta, or risotto. For my grandmothers' and my mother's generation, a primo was mandatory. And still, if you serve a small plate of pasta or risotto before you bring out the main course, it will always make your meal feel more formal and more celebratory (people love it). If I'm having even a smallish dinner party (ten people or fewer), I feel compelled to serve a first course because my training insists on it; I just don't feel like there's enough food otherwise!

But for everyday dining, I always advocate convenience: my students are used to eating main-course-size portions of primi as the main course, and so are Jack and I. While all the dishes in this chapter can be served in smaller quantities as first courses, I have planned them as entrées. Even the soups can double as a light meal. It's great to have soup in the house. Freeze it in 2-cup containers and you can put together a quick lunch or light dinner in minutes.

CHICKEN BROTH

MAKES ABOUT 3 QUARTS

	Fresh 5- to 6-pound fowl
12 CUPS	*cold water*
1	*medium yellow onion, peeled and left whole*
1	*carrot, peeled and cut in half*
1 STALK	*celery, cut in half*
¾ TEASPOON	*salt*
	KITCHEN STUFF
	A skimmer

ABOUT YOUR KITCHEN STUFF

A skimmer—a round, flat, mesh "spoon"—is very helpful when you're making broth. It makes it easy to lift the scum off the top and leave all the broth in the pot.

Nonna Stella kept chickens in her backyard in Piacenza. Every morning, she'd go out to the coop in the backyard and bring back eggs for breakfast. (If you've ever tasted eggs that fresh, you know how delicious they are.) While my brother and I watched Nonna frying or scrambling, we waited for my grandfather to arrive so that they could play their egg game.

"How old is this egg?" she'd ask.

"Oh, about ten minutes old," he'd say.

"Tsk, tsk," she'd say, shaking her head. "Do you have anything fresher?"

And we'd crack up.

When the chickens got too old to be good egg layers, my grandmother made them into the most full-bodied chicken broth ever. And like any grandmother's chicken soup, her "pastina in brodo" (see the sidebar on page 41) was a cure for most any ailment.

I don't have chickens, or even a backyard, but I usually do have chicken broth. And while canned stock is perfectly adequate for lots of things—most soups, stews, sauces—homemade broth is great to have on hand for chicken soup (add pastina or skinny angel hair pasta) and, especially, for risotto.

Broth is traditionally made with an older bird, called a fowl. Fowl have more flavor than chickens. They're also much tougher. Too tough to roast. But after simmering for two and a half hours, the meat is perfectly tender. If I don't serve the meat the day I make the broth, hot out of the pot, I'll chill it, tear it apart, and mix it into a green salad or use it for sandwiches.

When my mom cooks chicken or capon, she freezes the necks, gizzards and hearts in a resealable freezer bag. When it's time to cook stock, they add terrific flavor; add them to the pot with the fowl.

USE KITCHEN SHEARS to cut the fowl in half through the breast and backbone. Wrap one half in a freezer bag, and freeze it for up to 2 months, until you're ready to make broth again or bollito misto (page 135). Rinse the other half under cold, running water and dry it carefully with paper towels to remove any blood. Put the fowl in a large stockpot. Add the water, place the pot over medium-high heat, and bring to a simmer. Set a bowl next to the stove. As the water heats, the fat and a bunch of gray scum will gradually float to the top. Skim it off with a skimmer or a large spoon, putting it into the bowl. This will take 15 or 20 minutes of intermittent skimming.

When the water reaches a simmer and you've removed as much of the scum as you can, add the vegetables and the salt. Reduce the heat so that the water simmers very gently. Cover and simmer 2½ hours. Lift the lid every so often to skim the little bit of scum and fat that will continue to rise.

Remove the pot from the heat and let cool for a few minutes. Transfer the chicken and vegetables to a plate, using a slotted spoon or skimmer, and set them aside.

Line a mesh strainer with a damp paper towel and place over a large bowl. Carefully pour the broth through the strainer into the bowl. The fat will settle on the paper towel.

If you'd like to serve the broth for dinner, as I do, ladle some of it into a saucepan (enough soup for however many people you're feeding). Chop up the vegetables, and add them to the pan. Pull the meat off the bones and serve some of it with the soup. Refrigerate any leftover meat for sandwiches or salad.

To store the rest of the broth, let it cool slightly, then pour it into plastic containers. Refrigerate whatever you think you might use within the next 3 days, and freeze the rest.

THE TWIST

Fowl are apparently a little old-fashioned, like Nonna Stella's chicken coop, and not all supermarkets carry them regularly. You can order one or substitute the same weight in chicken leg quarters.

NONNA STELLA'S PASTINA IN BRODO

Bring 2 quarts chicken broth to a simmer in a saucepan. Add 1 cup pastina, cover, and simmer gently until the pastina is tender, 3 to 4 minutes. Serves 4, as a first course.

MINESTRONE

SERVES 4 TO 6

2 TABLESPOONS	*unsalted butter*
¼ CUP	*extra-virgin olive oil*
I	*large yellow onion, roughly chopped*
3	*carrots*
3 STALKS	*celery*
2	*large cloves garlic, smashed with the heel of your hand and peeled*
	Salt and freshly ground pepper
I	*large Idaho potato*
I ½ CUPS	*chopped, drained, canned tomatoes*
2 TABLESPOONS	*chopped fresh Italian parsley*
I POUND	*green beans, both ends trimmed*
½ BUNCH	*medium asparagus, ends trimmed*
2	*medium-size, firm zucchini (ends trimmed), cut in half lengthwise, halves sliced crosswise ⅓-inch thick and coarsely chopped*
I QUART	*low-sodium chicken broth*
I (14½ OUNCE) CAN	*cannellini beans, drained and rinsed*
½ CUP	*finely grated Parmesan cheese (optional)*

This is a turn-out-your-refrigerator soup. The traditional recipe, as I learned it, is made with onion, celery, carrots, garlic, green beans, potato, zucchini, asparagus, and cannellini beans. But I add other vegetables if I find them hiding in the refrigerator. My favorites are cubed squash (8 to 10 ounces; add it to the pot with the potato), spinach (5 ounces, roughly chopped), and basil (4 or 5 leaves, sliced)—both go in with the cannellini beans. And kidney beans work just as well as cannellini.

You'll see that I like my minestrone chunky. If you find that you want a brothier consistency, increase the broth by a cup or two.

IN A LARGE, HEAVY-BOTTOMED SOUP POT, heat the butter and olive oil over medium-low heat. Add the onion and cook 5 minutes without browning. (Lower the heat if the onion begins to turn golden.)

Slice the carrots and celery about ¼ inch thick. Add to the pot along with the garlic. Sprinkle with 1 teaspoon salt and ½ teaspoon pepper and cook until the vegetables begin to soften, about 15 minutes.

Peel the potato and cut it into ¼-inch cubes. Add to the pot along with the tomatoes and parsley. Cover and simmer very gently over low heat for 10 minutes.

Cut the green beans and asparagus into ¾- to 1-inch lengths, and add to the pot. Add the zucchini and chicken broth, and cover the pot. When the soup returns to a simmer, set a timer for 40 minutes.

When the timer goes off, add the cannellini beans, and cook 10 more minutes.

If you are using the cheese, stir it in or ladle the soup into bowls and sprinkle the cheese on top. Store leftovers in the refrigerator, or ladle into smaller containers and freeze.

THE TWIST

We Boiardis eat a lot of Parmesan cheese. Never one to waste anything, my grandmother always saved the rind, the hard, plasticky part on the outside of the cheese. She cooked it with the minestrone for flavor and body. (For free.) I usually buy already grated Parmesan, which means no rinds. I stir the grated cheese into the soup to get the same taste, but if you find yourself with a chunk of cheese, cut off the rind, wash it, and slip it into the pot after you add the green beans and asparagus.

DON'T TWIST LIKE *THAT!*

The vegetables in minestrone are all cut to the size of the cannellini beans, and added in stages because some take longer to cook than others. When I was in college, I tried streamlining the recipe so that I wouldn't have to do all that chopping: I cut the vegetables into big chunks. I tossed them into the pot. I added a bouillon cube and water. It simmered. I pureed. How easy was that? Well, I was terribly disappointed. The soup just didn't taste right. It wasn't minestrone. Sometimes the traditional is the Traditional for a reason.

BUTTERNUT SQUASH SOUP

SERVES 6 TO 8

I love this soup, as I love anything made with butternut squash. It's very light, flavored with a smidgeon of cumin.

The packaged, cleaned squash sold almost everywhere these days works perfectly here. If your market doesn't package it in the 20-ounce containers mine carries, a few ounces here or there won't make a huge difference. Or you can buy more than you need and roast the extra (page 160).

FOR EITHER VARIETY OF WHOLE SQUASH, cut the squash in half through the stem end with a big knife. Scrape out the seeds. Cut the squash into 2-inch cubes and cut off the skin with the knife.

In a large, heavy-bottomed soup pot, heat the olive oil over medium-low heat. Add the onion, ¾ teaspoon salt, and ⅛ teaspoon pepper and cook until the onion softens, 5 to 7 minutes. (Turn the heat down if the onion begins to brown.)

Add the carrots, celery, garlic, and cumin and stir with a wooden spoon so that everything is coated with the oil. Cook 1 to 2 minutes so that the oil has a chance to pick up the flavor of the garlic.

Add the cubed squash. Turn up the heat to medium-high. Cook, uncovered, stirring every now and again, until the edges of the vegetables begin to brown and you see brown bits beginning to stick to the bottom of the pan, 10 to 15 minutes. Check often to make sure that those brown bits don't burn, and scrape the bottom often. Turn down the heat if it gets too brown.

Stir in the broth, scraping the bottom of the pan to pick up any browned bits. Cover, and bring the soup to a gentle simmer. Cook until the vegetables are very soft, about 1 hour 15 minutes.

Working in batches, ladle the soup into a blender (fill the blender no more than halfway) and puree until very smooth. Pour the soup into a clean pot. If you want to thin it, rinse the blender with a little water or chicken broth, and add it to the pot. Bring to a simmer, taste for salt and pepper. Ladle into soup bowls. Store leftovers in the refrigerator, or freeze in smaller containers.

1	(2½-pound) butternut or kabocha squash, or 2 (20-ounce) packages cleaned, cubed butternut squash
5 TABLESPOONS	extra-virgin olive oil
1	onion, cut into 1-inch chunks
¾ TEASPOON	salt
⅛ TEASPOON	freshly ground pepper
2	carrots, cut into 1-inch chunks
3 STALKS	celery (preferably inner stalks), cut into 1-inch chunks
3 CLOVES	garlic, sliced
½ TEASPOON	ground cumin
4 CUPS	canned low-sodium chicken broth, or as needed

RISOTTO

Risotto is and always has been extremely popular in my family. We eat it all year round, in all sorts of different combinations: sometimes it's as simple as rice, onion, white wine, chicken broth, and cheese; sometimes we make it more elaborately with lobster, mushrooms, or asparagus. Personally I love it in all forms (though my favorite is mushroom). Once you get the hang of the Parmesan risotto on page 47, the others are essentially variations.

Risotto is made with a special, short-grain Italian rice. There are several varieties—we use either arborio (that you can find in the rice aisle of your supermarket) or carnaroli (that you'll find at an Italian specialty store). Broth is added to the rice little by little, and the rice is stirred as it cooks. The stirring gradually dissolves the starch from the rice into the hot broth, so that the risotto comes out creamy. A tablespoon of butter and a handful of grated cheese go in at the end. It's scrumptious.

Risotto is simple to make. It just requires a lot of stirring—and a ladle, preferably a large one. You must stir *constantly* to give risotto its trademark creamy texture. Stirring risotto was one of the first things my mom trusted me to do on my own. When she cooks, she doesn't take her eyes off the food. Not for long, anyway. So she'd be stirring the risotto, watching how much broth evaporated and how the look of the rice changed, gauging when to add the next ladleful. I'd be kneeling on my chair at the stove next to her. The phone would ring. She'd put the spoon in my hand, and I'd keep stirring, watching the rice carefully as I'd seen her do, until she returned.

RISOTTO

WITH PARMESAN CHEESE

SERVES 4

I got married in what is certainly one of the most gorgeous spots on the face of the earth, the hotel Villa d'Este. The place has a lot to recommend it for a wedding. In addition to being stunning, there's a church nearby, getting there from the airport couldn't be easier, and all of my family live within an easy distance. But I think what really sold me on it was the risotto.

My mom and I had planned to visit several possible wedding locales, and the Villa d'Este was our first stop. Perched on the edge of Lake Como, the hotel itself is exquisite—every room. You don't know what you could possibly do to make them more beautiful. The grounds are like a wonderland. Imagine rocky, terraced gardens decorated with tiled arcades, fountains, and sculptures. The lawn is perfectly manicured, and there's a swimming pool that actually floats in the lake.

My mom and I had dinner and spent the night there. I'd heard that the food was good. It was *unbelievable*. One of the dishes we tried was the Champagne risotto, made pretty much like this recipe, using Champagne in place of white wine. *It was amazing.* It turns out that the Villa d'Este is known for some of the best risotto in Italy. (They put out a cookbook called *Tales of Risotto: 50 Recipes: Culinary Adventures from Villa d'Este*, with recipes from the Villa's chef, Luciano Parolari.) That Champagne risotto sealed the deal. The way my family loves risotto? My mom and I never even looked at another place.

The food is so good at the Villa that I believe that Jack and I managed to taste every single thing on the menu during the five days we were there for the wedding. We certainly tried; we just kept ordering room service. We'd have a couple of hours between events, and we'd look at each other and say, "I wonder what *this* kind of ravioli tastes like. . . . Let's order it!" No item was left untried. Unbelievably fun.

Whenever we're in Milan, we try to get back there, even if it's just for a meal. Last time we were in Milan, the flight home was delayed ten hours. No problem—we hopped a cab and went to Lake Como for lunch.

IN A SAUCEPAN, bring the chicken broth to a bare simmer and adjust the heat so that the temperature remains constant; it should be nice and hot, but you don't want it to reduce. (So don't boil it.)

7 CUPS	chicken broth, preferably homemade (see page 40), or canned low-sodium broth
1½ TABLESPOONS	unsalted butter
1 TABLESPOON	extra-virgin olive oil
1	small yellow onion, chopped as finely as you can
	Salt
2 CUPS	arborio or carnaroli rice
½ CUP	dry white wine, such as Pinot Grigio
¼ CUP	finely grated Parmesan cheese, plus extra for serving
	Freshly ground pepper
	KITCHEN STUFF
	Large ladle

Cut off ½ tablespoon of the butter and put it into a 10- or 11-inch skillet, sauté pan, or casserole over low heat. Reserve the remaining tablespoon of butter. Add the olive oil and wait until the butter melts. Add the onion and ¼ teaspoon salt. Stir with a wooden spoon to coat the onion with the fat. Then let the onion cook, stirring once or twice, until it is very tender but not browned, 8 to 10 minutes. This is important: the texture of risotto should be delicate—you don't want to taste hard pieces of onion in it, and the onion must not brown. Turn the heat down if you see it begin to go golden.

Add the rice and cook about 2 minutes, stirring well, until it is well coated with the fat and onion, and when you bend your nose toward the pan, the rice smells a little toasty. Pour the wine over the rice. Stir well, making sure to get into the sides of the pan to catch all the rice. Cook until the wine evaporates and the pan is dry (you'll hear the fat sizzle).

Add one large ladleful of the hot chicken broth to the pan, enough to just cover the rice. Stir well to incorporate and then continue stirring and cooking until the rice has absorbed all the broth. This will take 2 or 3 minutes. Adjust the heat so that the mixture simmers very gently, the bubbles lazily but continuously breaking the surface. Add another ladleful of broth, and continue with the stirring until once again, the broth is almost completely absorbed. Make sure to stir into the edges of the pan to reach all the rice so that it cooks evenly. Continue with this process, stirring constantly, until the rice is completely cooked through and tender, but with a little tooth; it shouldn't be at all mushy. You won't use all the broth. Add a last ladleful of broth, and immediately remove the pan from the heat. This broth-and-stirring process should take about 25 minutes in all and use about 6 cups broth. But don't be upset if you use more (that's what it's there for) or if it takes a little longer to cook. It'll taste great, regardless!

Add the reserved 1 tablespoon butter and the cheese and stir well to blend the rice with that last ladleful of broth, cheese, and butter, so that the risotto is nice and creamy. (If it's dry, you can add a touch more broth.) Let it rest for a few minutes. Then spoon the risotto onto plates, and sprinkle with a pinch of pepper and a little more Parmesan, if you like (I do). Eat the risotto right away while it's hot and creamy!

RISOTTO
WITH ASPARAGUS

SERVES 4

My mother occasionally still refers to recipes, but my grandmother never did. Nonna Stella didn't measure anything—not in the way we think of measuring. She calculated by hand and by eye. Risotto was one fistful of rice per person. She added broth by the ladleful—tasting constantly—until the texture of the risotto was right. This is a variation on Risotto with Parmesan Cheese (page 47), with bite-sized pieces of asparagus.

BRING A SAUCEPAN of salted water to a boil. Put a colander in the sink. Trim the ends from the asparagus. Cut the asparagus into ¾-inch lengths. Add the pieces to the boiling water and simmer until cooked about halfway (they won't be entirely tender), 2 to 3 minutes. Drain in the colander.

Follow steps 1 through 4 in the recipe for Parmesan risotto on page 47. But after the risotto has cooked 15 minutes, stir in the drained asparagus. Continue cooking as directed, stirring constantly, until the risotto is done. Add the final ladleful of stock, remove the pan from the heat, and stir in the reserved butter and cheese, as in step 5. Let rest for a few minutes, then serve sprinkled with a pinch of pepper and a little more Parmesan, if you like.

	Salt
1 POUND	medium asparagus
7 CUPS	chicken broth, preferably homemade (see page 40), or canned low-sodium broth
1½ TABLESPOONS	unsalted butter
1 TABLESPOON	extra-virgin olive oil
1	small yellow onion, chopped as finely as you can
2 CUPS	arborio or carnaroli rice
½ CUP	dry white wine, such as Pinot Grigio
¼ CUP	finely grated Parmesan cheese, plus extra for serving
	Freshly ground pepper

MY DAD'S SAFFRON RISOTTO

My dad loves saffron risotto, which we call Risotto Milanese. My grandfather loved it too, and the story is that my grandmother made it all the time for the two of them. But everybody else in my family prefers some other type of risotto, and my mom has given up making the saffron. So the poor man can't get his favorite risotto anymore. And he gets pretty upset about it. "None of you understands what good food is," he grumbles. The last time my mom broke down and made it for him, he kidded her, "What's wrong, is someone dying? I haven't seen this dish in years." So this is for you, Dad.

Make the risotto as in the basic recipe, adding two .075-gram envelopes, or ⅛ teaspoon, saffron to the broth as it heats.

RISOTTO

WITH PORCINI MUSHROOMS

SERVES 4

Another variation on Risotto with Parmesan Cheese (page 47), this one is flavored with dried porcini mushrooms. Italians don't think of dried porcinis as a compromise (as in, we'd really rather be eating fresh, but we'll settle for the dried). They're just different. Fresh porcinis are *sooo* out of this world! No question. But the dried mushrooms have a wonderfully intense flavor and smell that I love. And unlike the fresh ones, they'll last practically forever in the freezer. In fact, if you've got the mushrooms and the basics in your pantry and fridge, there's nothing here that requires a trip to the supermarket.

The mushrooms are soaked in boiling water for an hour to reconstitute them. This soaking also creates a broth that adds even more flavor to the risotto. So don't throw away the broth when you strain the mushrooms!

IN A SMALL SAUCEPAN, bring the water to a boil. Remove from the heat, add the dried mushrooms, and let stand at least 1 hour; the mushrooms should be soft and plump, and you should feel no hard areas when you press them between your fingers. Set a fine strainer over a bowl. Strain the mushrooms, reserving the soaking liquid. Rinse the mushrooms in the strainer under cold running water. Pat dry on paper towels. Coarsely chop and set aside. Line the fine strainer with paper towels. Strain the mushroom broth into another bowl to remove any grit. You'll have about 1 cup broth; set it aside in a measuring cup.

Follow steps 1 through 4 for the Parmesan risotto on page 47, using 2 tablespoons of the butter and the olive oil to cook the onion. After the risotto has cooked 15 minutes, stir in chopped mushrooms. Stir in the mushroom broth, ¼ cup at a time, cooking and stirring until it is completely evaporated before adding the next ¼ cup. (After you've made this a couple of times, you may decide you want to add less mushroom broth. It's all about personal taste, anyway.)

Continue adding the broth as before, stirring constantly, until the risotto is done. Add the final ladleful of broth, remove the pan from the heat, and stir in the remaining 1 tablespoon butter and the cheese, as in step 5. Let rest for a few minutes. Then spoon the risotto onto plates, and sprinkle with a pinch of pepper and a little more Parmesan.

2 CUPS	water
1 OUNCE	dried porcini mushrooms, preferably Italian
6 CUPS	chicken broth, preferably homemade (see page 40), or canned low-sodium broth
3 TABLESPOONS	unsalted butter
2 TABLESPOONS	extra-virgin olive oil
½	yellow onion, chopped as finely as you can
	Salt
2 CUPS	arborio or carnaroli rice
½ CUP	dry white wine, such as Pinot Grigio
¼ CUP	finely grated Parmesan cheese, plus extra for serving
	Freshly ground pepper

SHOPPING WITH ANNA

Dried porcinis are sold by weight in specialty food stores. The best ones are imported from Italy and sold in grams: 28 grams = 1 ounce. Wrap them well and store them in the freezer.

LOBSTER RISOTTO

SERVES 4

2 TABLESPOONS	*extra-virgin olive oil*
I TABLESPOON	*finely chopped shallot*
I CLOVE	*garlic, finely chopped*
15	*cherry tomatoes*
I POUND	*raw shelled lobster meat, cut into ½-inch pieces*
½ CUP	*dry white wine, such as Pinot Grigio*
8 CUPS	*chicken broth, preferably homemade (page 40), or canned low-sodium broth*
I ½ TABLESPOONS	*unsalted butter*
I	*small onion, chopped as finely as you can*
	Salt and freshly ground pepper
2 CUPS	*arborio or carnaroli rice*
I TABLESPOON	*chopped fresh Italian parsley*
	Finely grated zest of ½ lemon

In America, many Italian families celebrate a tradition of the Feast of Seven Fishes on New Year's Eve, a meatless meal made up of seven (or sometimes eight, or nine) different seafood dishes. That tradition seems to have originated in southern Italy; in any event, our family never followed it.

Boiardis did, however, always sit down to a meatless meal on that night. My grandparents would eat a dish of salt cod called baccalà (page 37) and perhaps saltwater eel, marinated in vinegar and bay leaf (you can still buy it readymade in Piacenza). In America, my mom would serve the baccalà or some other fish, along with a meatless pasta, gnocchi with tomato sauce, or this lobster risotto.

Ask at your fish store or supermarket seafood counter for shelled lobster meat.

IN A 9- OR 10-INCH SKILLET, heat 1 tablespoon of the olive oil over medium-low heat. Add the shallot and cook, stirring every now and then, until translucent, 5 to 7 minutes. (Turn the heat down if it begins to brown.) Add the garlic and cook 2 more minutes. Add the cherry tomatoes and cook until softened, 8 to 10 minutes.

Add the lobster meat and stir well. Add ¼ cup of the wine and cook until evaporated. Add 1 cup of the broth, bring to a simmer, and simmer gently until the lobster is cooked through, 10 to 12 minutes. Remove the pan from the heat; set aside.

Meanwhile, bring the rest of your 7 cups broth to a simmer in a saucepan, as in step 1 of the Risotto with Parmesan Cheese (page 47). Follow steps 2 through 4, but about 5 minutes before the risotto is cooked, add the reserved lobster mixture to the skillet. Continue cooking as in step 4, stirring constantly, until the risotto is done. Add the final ladleful of broth, remove the skillet from the heat, and follow step 5 to stir in the reserved 1 tablespoon butter. Stir in the chopped parsley, and lemon zest. (No Parmesan in this risotto.) Let the risotto rest 2 minutes before serving.

GNOCCHI

Gnocchi just means "dumplings," and Italians make lots of different types, depending on where you grow up. Potato gnocchi (page 54), for example, were traditionally a northern dish; these days, they're made all over Italy. Pisarei (page 60), made with bread crumbs, are still found only in the area around Piacenza; chicchi (made with potato, ricotta cheese, and spinach) are another dumpling specialty from my hometown (page 64).

As you travel south in Italy, gnocchi ingredients and methods change. In Rome, for example, gnocchi alla Romana are made with semolina and milk and eggs, and shaped into disks. But that's not our territory, and we don't make them.

I've given some traditional pairings of gnocchi and sauce in this chapter, but you can mix and match with the sauces in the book: Uncle Hector's Tomato Sauce (page 80), sage butter (page 98), and Bolognese sauce (page 92). Or just melted butter and Parmesan cheese. Yum.

POTATO GNOCCHI

WITH PESTO

SERVES 4 TO 6 AS AN ENTRÉE

	GNOCCHI
6	6-ounce medium Idaho potatoes, unpeeled
	Salt
I	large egg yolk
2 CUPS PLUS 2 TABLESPOONS	all-purpose flour
	PESTO
2 CUPS	firmly packed basil leaves, preferably small leaves
½ CUP	extra-virgin olive oil
2 TABLESPOONS	pine nuts
½ TEASPOON	salt
½ CLOVE	garlic
3 TABLESPOONS	finely grated Parmesan cheese, plus extra for serving
2 TABLESPOONS	finely grated pecorino cheese
3 TABLESPOONS	heavy cream
PINCH	freshly ground pepper
	KITCHEN STUFF
	Slotted spoon or wire mesh spider, available at Asian cooking supply stores
	Potato ricer

I didn't get the hang of gnocchi making until sometime in my early teens. For years, I watched my mother make them, and it always looked so *easy* in her hands. When I tried it, I'd get these shapeless blobs. "Push down harder, *cic*," she'd say (that's pronounced "CHEECH," short for *cicetti*, an affectionate term—something like little sweetheart), and then . . . "No, not *too* hard!" And always, "You have to go a little faster."

Gnocchi do require some practice and dexterity, and when I got a little proficient at making them, it was a real milestone in my cooking career. My mom still talks about it: the day I mastered gnocchi was the day I truly became a help to her in the kitchen. And I began to feel pride that I could make a contribution to the household aside from setting the table and spinning lettuce. Now the two of us can bang out a batch of these little delicacies in a little over an hour. Good thing; I adore them.

My niece and nephew get a kick out of making gnocchi, too. They put on aprons and sit at the kitchen counter with my mom—pretty impressive for a five-year-old and an eight-year-old. She gives them each a piece of the dough, and they roll it into ropes and cut it into pieces, just like they're playing with Play-Doh. When the gnocchi are cooked and sauced, they're very proud of their handiwork (and we don't tell them otherwise).

Potato gnocchi freeze very well: shape them, stick them (on the floured baking sheet) in the freezer until they're frozen hard, then dump them into freezer bags. When you're ready to eat, cook the still-frozen gnocchi in boiling water just as if they were fresh. Gnocchi last several months in the freezer.

Potato gnocchi are traditionally served with tomato sauce (page 80), Bolognese sauce (page 92), or sage butter (page 98), but I like them best with pesto, a finely chopped mixture of fresh basil, garlic, and Parmesan cheese. Some pestos are chunky; I like mine ultimately smooth—the texture of a *sauce* rather than a chopped condiment—and we add a little cream to smooth it out even further. My students love pesto because it's super easy: throw all the ingredients into the food processor and press the button.

The best pesto is made from small, mild-tasting young basil leaves. It lasts well for a couple of days in the refrigerator, but it freezes well too. Spoon it into ice cube trays and freeze; then put the pesto "cubes" into a freezer bag. We use pesto on so many things: Caprese salad, panini, pasta, a dollop on top of deviled eggs, or on bruschetta. And it's great on sandwiches.

My mom makes five or six times the recipe when she finds good basil. I don't go that far, but I sometimes envy her those cubes of pesto in the freezer.

TO MAKE THE GNOCCHI, put the potatoes in a large pot. Add cold water to cover and 1 tablespoon salt. Bring the water to a boil, turn the heat down so that the water just simmers, cover, and cook the potatoes 30 minutes. (Don't get curious and poke the potatoes with a knife or fork while they cook. If you puncture the skin, the flesh will get watery and absorb too much flour, which makes the gnocchi heavy.) Remove the cooked potatoes to a plate with a slotted spoon or spider and let them sit until cool enough to handle, about 10 minutes. Peel the potatoes with a small knife—the skin will slip off easily.

Set a cutting board on your work surface. Press the peeled potatoes through a ricer onto the cutting board. Use your hands to gently make a well in the center of the riced potato. Put the egg yolk in the well and sprinkle with 1 teaspoon salt. Using a spoon or clean hands, sprinkle the potato evenly with the flour.

With a fork, beat the salt and egg together. Little by little, begin drawing the potato-flour mixture into the center of the well with the fork, and work it into the egg until the egg mixture becomes too stiff to work with the fork. Use your fingertips to gently draw the rest of the potato mixture into the center and mash it all together with your fingertips to make a rough dough. Gather the dough into a ball and fold it over on itself several times, gently kneading, until the dough is well blended, soft, and smooth. This will take just a few minutes. Shape the dough into a log 12 to 14 inches long and 4 inches wide. Set it at the top of your board.

To shape the gnocchi, lightly flour a baking sheet and put it next to your cutting board. Use a pastry scraper or a knife to cut off a 1- to 1½-inch wide chunk of dough. Roll the dough between your hands on the cutting board to make a rope about ¾ inch thick. Cut the rope into 1-inch lengths (each of these will be a gnoccho). Lightly flour the tines of the fork. Hold the fork with your left hand so that the tines are almost flat against the board. Place a piece of dough across the tines of the fork, close to the handle. With your right thumb, mash it against the tines while rolling it down and away from the handle. It will roll over

on itself so that instead of being plump and smooth, it will be curled, with an indentation from your thumb. Set the finished gnoccho on the floured baking sheet. Continue just like this to shape all of the gnocchi from your rope.

Cut, roll, and shape more gnocchi, until you've used all the dough. As you get adept at the shaping, you'll get more of an assembly-line thing going: roll three ropes at a time, cut them all into pieces, and shape them all into gnocchi. Just like that. I promise.

TO MAKE THE PESTO, combine the basil, olive oil, pine nuts, and salt in a blender. Cut the garlic into pieces and add it to the blender. Blend until the mixture is smooth and creamy, and you don't see any more large pieces of basil. Scrape the pesto into a medium bowl. Stir in the cheeses and then the cream, 1 tablespoon at a time. Stir in the pepper.

To cook the gnocchi, bring a large pot of water to a boil and add enough salt to make the water taste salty (about ¼ cup). Set a colander in a bowl, and place next to the stove. Add half of the gnocchi to the boiling water; when they rise to the surface, set your timer to 2 minutes. Use a slotted spoon or spider to remove the gnocchi to the colander when done; let drain. Transfer to a bowl. Return the water to a boil, add the rest of the gnocchi, and cook and drain the same way. Don't pour out the cooking water yet.

To serve, spoon about half of the pesto onto a large serving platter and stir in a spoonful of the pasta cooking water (this will thin the pesto). Spoon the gnocchi on top in an even layer. Spoon the rest of the pesto over the gnocchi, and gently toss with the spoon so that the gnocchi are entirely coated with the pesto. Sprinkle all over, very lightly and evenly, with more Parmesan cheese, and serve.

THE TWIST

The Italian formula for potato gnocchi is simple: 1 kilo (a little more than 2 pounds) potatoes, 300 grams flour (about 10½ ounces), and a little salt. Period. But American potatoes are moister than their Italian counterparts, so in America, we add one egg yolk per recipe to "stick" the moist dough together.

There's a reason for the traditional shape of potato gnocchi (it's not just to make more work and drive us crazy!): the indentations catch and hold the sauce better than a smooth dumpling would. But even in Italy, cooks don't always do this step anymore. They just roll the dough into ropes, cut it into pieces, and cook it. You can do that, if you like—because they're thicker, you'll need to cook these plumper gnocchi for about 4 minutes instead of 2.

PISAREI E FASO

SERVES 4

FASO	
1 (32-OUNCE) CAN	imported Italian plum tomatoes
¼ CUP	extra-virgin olive oil
3 TABLESPOONS	unsalted butter
1	onion, chopped
2	large, fresh sage leaves
	Needles from a 4-inch sprig fresh rosemary, or ½ teaspoon dried rosemary
	Salt and freshly ground pepper
1 POUND	fresh cranberry or other fresh shell beans, shelled and rinsed, or (14-ounce) can borlotti or red beans, drained
1 TABLESPOON	chopped fresh Italian parsley
PISAREI	
1¼ CUPS	dried, seasoned bread crumbs
1¼ CUPS	all-purpose flour
½ TO ¾ CUP	finely grated Parmesan cheese, for serving
KITCHEN STUFF	
	A large, pretty shallow serving bowl

If there's one recipe that's typical of my family's hometown, it's these bite-sized bread dumplings served in tomato sauce with cranberry beans. You'll find this dish made throughout the area around Piacenza, in home kitchens and restaurants, but not so much in the rest of Italy. And I've never seen it on a menu in the States.

You can tell the age of the dish by its name: *pisarei* means "pasta" in the ancient regional dialect of Piacenza; *faso* means "beans." Although its uniqueness has given it the cachet of a regional specialty, traditionally it was peasant food—cheap, hearty, and filling. The dumplings are made from dried bread crumbs mixed to a stiff dough with flour and water and shaped by hand, like potato gnocchi.

My grandfather and his brothers made a point of returning to Piacenza with their families at least once a year. For one day of the visit, they reserved a long table at La Croce Bianca, where my grandfather and Uncle Hector had learned to cook as boys. Friends and family dropped by for a daylong feast that always included pisarei.

By local standards, the pisarei and beans should resemble each other in size so much as to be indistinguishable when you put them in your mouth. As a child, I hated beans; I used to sit at the dinner table, fork in hand, pressing on each of the "bumps" to determine which were the dumplings and which were the dreaded beans. I love the dish now, not just because it's delicious but because it inevitably reminds me of home. I make a big batch of the dumplings when I have the time and freeze them in resealable plastic bags. It's like having store-bought, frozen pasta in the freezer, but better.

Our family sauce recipe is made with a 32-ounce can of tomatoes, which I buy at a specialty market. If you can't find the 32-ounce size, a 28-ounce can (available at your supermarket) will work just fine.

FOR THE FASO, set a food mill over a large bowl. Dump the whole can of tomatoes, with their juices, into the food mill and work the tomatoes through until all that's left in the mill is a handful of dryish tomato pulp with seeds. Discard the pulp and seeds.

Put the oil and butter into a medium saucepan, set it over low heat, and heat until a little piece of onion sizzles when you toss it into the pan. Add the chopped onion and cook until translucent but not brown, 8 to 10 minutes.

Chop together the sage and fresh rosemary, if using. Add them, along with 1 teaspoon salt, to the onions, and cook a few minutes longer. (If using dried rosemary, add at the same time as you would add the fresh rosemary.)

Add the pureed tomato. Bring the mixture to a simmer and cook 10 minutes. Add the fresh beans, if using, cover, and cook until they are a little squishy when you press them between thumb and forefinger, 40 to 45 minutes. (If you're using canned beans, add them during the last 10 minutes of cooking.) Remove the sauce from the heat, and stir in the parsley. Set the sauce aside.

FOR THE PISAREI, bring a small saucepan of water to a boil. Put the bread crumbs into a large bowl. When the water comes to a boil, turn it down to a simmer. Measure out ⅓ cup simmering water. Pour it over the bread crumbs and stir with a fork to moisten. Then add another ⅓ cup simmering water, and stir and mash to incorporate it. Add more simmering water, about 2 tablespoons at a time, until the mixture holds together and there are no more loose, dry crumbs (you'll use about ⅞ cup water total). Let the dough cool just until it's no longer hot to the touch.

Lightly flour a work surface. Add about half of the flour to the bowl with the bread-crumb mixture and stir and mash that in with your fork. Add the rest of the flour; the mixture will now be too stiff to stir. Use clean hands to press it together to form a shaggy dough. Don't worry if some of the flour doesn't incorporate. Turn the dough out of the bowl and knead it a few times on your work surface until it comes together into a fairly smooth ball. Put a baking sheet next to the bowl and dust it with flour.

To shape the pisarei, pull off a hunk of dough and roll it on your floured work surface into a rope as thick as your index finger. Cut the rope into ½-inch lengths. Working with one piece at a time, press down on the dough with your right thumb, dragging your thumb across it so that the dough flattens and rolls around the thumb: it should look like a small shell. Place on the baking sheet. Continue this way to make the rest of the pisarei. (At this point, you can cover the baking sheet with plastic and put it in the freezer. When the pisarei are

THE TWIST (SORT OF)

This yummy, cranberry-bean-studded tomato sauce is also traditionally served with tagliatelle, so I tell my students not to wait to try it; make the time-consuming pisarei when you have time. Make the sauce when you need dinner.

A family dinner at La Croce Bianca, Piacenza, Italy, 1970.

frozen, transfer them to resealable plastic bags and store them in the freezer for up to 2 months.)

To serve, bring a large pot of water to a boil. Add enough salt to make the water taste salty (about ¼ cup). Put a colander in the sink. Meanwhile, warm the faso gently over low heat. Add the pisarei to the boiling water. When they float to the top, set the timer for 7 minutes, and cook until the pisarei are tender and the floury taste has been cooked out. You may need to cook for a minute or so longer after the timer goes off. Drain in the colander, and transfer to a serving bowl. Spoon the sauce over the pisarei, sprinkle with a good handful of Parmesan, and stir well. Sprinkle with more cheese and serve in shallow bowls.

POLENTA

SERVES 6

Polenta has become rather chic in America, but in Italy, it's peasant food—inexpensive, filling, and versatile. The polenta (cornmeal) is cooked in boiling water until it turns into a creamy porridge. It can be served just like that as a primo, with a little Parmesan cheese or tomato sauce. We also serve it with saucy, main course dishes such as chicken cacciatore (page 125) or brasato (page 141), or just as we would serve pasta—topped with tomato sauce (page 80) and grated cheese, with Bolognese (page 92) or mushroom sauce (page 84). And it becomes something *really* irresistible when you layer it—like polenta pasticciata—with tomato sauce and cheese (page 132).

The trick to smooth, creamy polenta is to add the polenta to the water *off* the heat, stirring constantly. Then it practically makes itself.

You'll find polenta in specialty stores that sell Italian ingredients. It may be labeled "polenta flour"—it's the same thing.

8 CUPS	*water*
1 TABLESPOON	*salt*
2 CUPS	*polenta*
	Unsalted butter for the baking dish or bowl

BRING THE WATER TO A ROLLING BOIL over high heat in a large saucepan. Add the salt and boil for about 15 seconds. Remove the pan from the heat and reduce the heat to low. Off the heat, slowly pour in the polenta, stirring constantly with a long-handled wooden spoon until smooth. Return the pan to the heat and bring the polenta to a slow boil. Adjust the heat so that big, lazy bubbles break the surface every several seconds. Cook, stirring now and then to keep the polenta from sticking and burning on the bottom of the pot, until it thickens enough to pull away from the sides of the pan, it tastes cooked, and the texture is smooth and light, 35 to 40 minutes.

Smear the bottom and sides of an 8-inch square baking dish or a serving bowl with butter, and pour in the finished polenta.

CHICCHI DEL NONNO

SERVES 4

	CHICCHI
I (8-OUNCE) CONTAINER	whole-milk ricotta cheese (you'll need ½ cup plus 2 tablespoons, drained)
3	Idaho potatoes, about 1⅓ pounds total
2 CUPS	tightly packed spinach (not baby spinach), tough stems broken off
	Salt
I CUP PLUS 3 TABLESPOONS	all-purpose flour, plus extra for rolling
I	large egg (you'll use the yolk and about half the white)
	SAUCE
	1 recipe Uncle Hector's Tomato Sauce (page 80)
2 TABLESPOONS	heavy cream
¼ TO ⅓ CUP	finely grated Parmesan cheese
	KITCHEN STUFF
	Slotted spoon or spider
	Potato ricer

Chicchi (pronounced "KEE kee") are another dumpling from our area. They are smaller than potato gnocchi—about the size of a coffee bean. The traditional recipe (which we like) is made with a combination of potato, ricotta cheese, and spinach, but the formula has evolved in the area around Piacenza: sometimes the spinach is replaced by asparagus, sometimes by butternut squash.

The process for making chicchi is very similar to making potato gnocchi. The dough itself is a little trickier because the ricotta makes it wetter, and it's important not to add too much flour (the chicchi will be tough). They're easier to shape, though—just roll and cut.

You'll need to drain the ricotta for the dough overnight in the refrigerator to get rid of some of the water. Since it's hard to know exactly how much undrained cheese will equal the drained amount required, drain an entire 8-ounce container. You'll use most of that, and whatever you have left will be delicious tossed with pasta and tomato sauce later on.

Chicchi are traditionally served with a lightly creamed tomato sauce.

FOR THE CHICCHI, line a fine strainer with a double layer of paper towels and set the strainer over a bowl. Scrape the ricotta into the strainer, cover with plastic wrap and refrigerate overnight to drain.

Put the potatoes in a saucepan. Add cold water to cover. Bring to a boil, reduce the heat and simmer, partially covered, 30 minutes. Do not puncture the potato skins with a fork or knife while the potatoes cook. Drain and set the potatoes aside for about 10 minutes (until cool enough to handle).

Meanwhile, put the spinach in a large bowl of cold water and swish the leaves in the bowl several times to wash. Lift the spinach out of the water and spin it quickly in a salad spinner (the leaves will still be a little wet; that's fine). Put the spinach in a saucepan. Add ¼ teaspoon salt. Place the pan over low heat, cover it, and cook until the spinach is wilted and tender, 5 to 8 minutes. Hold a fine strainer over the pan, lift the cooked spinach into the strainer with a fork and press down to squeeze as much liquid as you can from the spinach. Put the spinach on a large cutting board and finely chop.

Measure ½ cup plus 2 tablespoons of the drained ricotta; set aside. Refrigerate what's left over for another use.

When the potatoes are cool, peel them with a small knife. Press them through a ricer and onto the cutting board with the spinach. Use clean hands to combine the potato and spinach a bit. Then make a well in the center of the potato-spinach mixture. Add the drained ricotta to the center of the well. Use the fork to mash the ricotta. Gradually pull the potato mixture into the well and gently mash it all together with the fork until roughly combined.

Make a well again in the new mixture. Sprinkle the 1 cup plus 3 tablespoons flour all over the potato mixture. Break the egg, and add the yolk and about half of the white to the center of the well. Add a scant teaspoon salt. Beat with the fork to blend the egg, then begin pulling the potato mixture into the center of the well with the fork. The mixture will soon become too stiff to work effectively with the fork. Set the fork aside, and begin gently kneading the mixture with clean hands, mashing it together with your fingers, folding it over on itself, and then mashing some more. When you have made a rough dough, scrape up any flour and wet dough that's stuck to the board, and incorporate that into the dough too. You're done when the dough comes together into a neat, damp-but-not-sticky ball. Flatten the ball into an oblong and set it at the top of your board.

You're ready to shape the chicchi now. Lightly flour a baking sheet. Put about ¼ cup flour on the side of your cutting board. Sweep some of it onto the center of the board to dust lightly. Cut off a piece of dough and roll it on the floured board, between two hands, to make a long rope, ½ to ¾ inch thick. Use a knife to cut ½-inch pieces. (These are the chicchi—they should be about the size of those pastel-colored mints you find in glass bowls at the cashier's desk at diners.) Place the chicchi in a single layer on the baking sheet. Cut another piece of dough, sweep some more of the flour onto the cutting board, and roll and cut more chicchi. When you've covered the bottom of the baking sheet with chicchi, cover that layer with a piece of parchment paper and make another layer. You should use all the flour for dusting, but try not to use more. The chicchi can now sit at room temperature for about 1 hour, or you can freeze them on the baking sheet; once they are frozen, dump them into a resealable plastic bag and put them back in the freezer until you want them.

Bring a wide shallow pot of water to a boil for the chicchi. Add enough salt to make the water taste salty (about ¼ cup). Set a colander on a deep plate (or in a shallow bowl) on the stove.

Bring the tomato sauce to a simmer. Add the cream, and remove the pan from the heat.

Add about half of the chicchi to the boiling water. When they float to the surface, set the timer for 2 minutes. Remove the cooked chicchi to the colander with a spider or slotted spoon. Add the rest of the chicchi to the water; you'll cook and drain them the same way.

While the second batch of chicchi cooks, spread some of the warm sauce over the bottom of a large, shallow serving bowl. Sprinkle all over with about 1 tablespoon of the Parmesan. Add the drained chicchi and spread them out evenly. Spoon more of the sauce over, gently nudging the chicchi so that they settle into the sauce. Sprinkle with another tablespoon of Parmesan. Drain the rest of the chicchi, dump them on top of the sauce, and gently spread them out. Spoon enough sauce over the top to cover (you'll have some sauce left over), and sprinkle with the remaining Parmesan. Pour the remaining sauce into a bowl. Serve the chicchi immediately with the sauce on the side.

THE TWIST

Before there were food processors, there were food mills, and they are a tradition I do not recommend "twisting." A food mill works better for tomato sauce than a food processor because it strains out the tomato seeds and any stray skin as it purées. Food mills are available at many supermarkets and at kitchen supply stores.

The tomatoes are a different story: In his Cleveland restaurant, Il Giardino, and in the Chef Boyardee factory, Uncle Hector made sauce with fresh tomatoes, but we make it with canned, which are not only more convenient, but more consistent. The best tomatoes are labeled "San Marzano" (a variety of plum tomato). Some supermarkets carry them; Italian specialty stores definitely will.

The spice, tang and sizzle of pepperoni pizza,

now in a mix.

This is pepperoni: Italian sausage with its own special seasonings. These lean, tender slices of pepperoni are filled with a lively, unique flavor that puts extra pep in pizza.

Only Chef Boy-Ar-Dee®, with his special skill and know-how, could make an authentic pepperoni pizza in a mix.

From Chef's mix you make a crispy, one-step crust that bakes up crunchy on the outside, tender in the middle. And there's a brand-new pizza sauce with 18 lively slices of pepperoni. Add Chef's cheese topping, bake, and in minutes... a sizzling pepperoni pizza. It's one of America's favorites.

Chef Boy-Ar-Dee

The party-time pizza with the crispy, one-step crust

Here's the easiest, tastest pizza mix that ever pepped up a party!

Chef Boy-Ar-Dee gives you a complete mix ... lots of grated cheese, rich, slow-simmered Italian pizza sauce, even yeast and flour already blended for a new, one-step crust. It's easy and

fun to fix—and bakes up in minutes while the party cooks, too. Before you know it, it's ready —oven-fresh, and as crisp and mouth-wateringly delicious as any pizza you've ever tasted anywhere.

Pizza time is fun time, so keep several boxes

on hand. Chef Boy-Ar-Dee Pizza. Two to choose from: cheese, or sausage with cheese. Yummmmm!

(P.S. You don't have to save Chef Pizza Mix for a party. Bake one up anytime pizza hunger strikes in your home.)

Chef Boy-Ar-Dee® Pizza Mix

Early advertising for Chef Boyardee's popular pizza kit.

NOW... TWO GREAT PIZZAS!

CHEF BOY-AR-DEE PIZZA WITH SAUSAGE COMPLETE WITH CHEESE

America's newest! It's a great new pizza treat, loaded with sausage in real pizza sauce. It's peppier. Richer. Every delicious bite has that exciting sausage-pizza flavor. Tender crunchy pizza crust and lots of Italian-style cheese. Comes complete in one box. Nothing else to buy. Ready for the oven in 15 minutes.

A meal in a minute with the

CHEF BOY-

CHEF BOY-AR-DEE PIZZA COMPLETE WITH CHEESE

America's favorite! It's pizza with true Italian pizza sauce. Lots of tangy cheese, too. And the crust! Crunchy outside . . . tender inside. You make it fast from box to oven in 15 minutes, bubbling hot and delicious. Only pennies a serving. No wonder Chef Boy-Ar-Dee outsells all other pizza mixes by more than 2 to 1.

Chef's touch in it.

AR-DEE®

PIZZA MARGHERITA

MAKES 2 PIZZAS, ENOUGH FOR 4 TO 6 EATERS

	PIZZA DOUGH
3 CUPS	all-purpose flour
1 TEASPOON	salt
½ TEASPOON	sugar
1 TEASPOON	fresh yeast, or 1 package active-dry yeast
1½ CUPS	warm water
2 TABLESPOONS	extra-virgin olive oil
	SAUCE
1 (28-OUNCE) CAN	plum tomatoes, drained, juice reserved
1½ TABLESPOONS	extra-virgin olive oil
1 CLOVE	garlic, pressed through a garlic press
PINCH	peperoncino (see sidebar page 90)
	Salt
1½ POUNDS	mozzarella cheese
15 LEAVES	fresh basil
	Olive oil, for the cookie sheet and for drizzling

Pizza is not traditionally from our part of Italy. My mother never even tasted it until she was fourteen or fifteen years old, at which point, she says, "I thought it was the best thing I'd ever eaten!"

Now of course you find pizza all over Italy, in restaurants called *pizzerie* (where you can also get antipasto, pastas, salads, and desserts to go along with the pizza). It used to be that the pizzas were always made in rounds just large enough for one person. Now the trend is to shape them into long oblongs and sell them by the slice, called *trancio*.

My mom wasn't one for canned foods (even Boiardi cans), but we all loved the Chef Boyardee pizza kit. It was easy enough for my brother and me to make on our own when we were young (with a little supervision from my mom). My memories of those afternoons are so delicious; I keep a Chef Boyardee pizza kit on the shelf over my stove because it makes me happy to look at it.

Mozzarella is the family favorite, but you can also top your pizza with grated Parmesan, pecorino, Fontina, or Swiss cheese, or a combination.

Pizza makes a great, great dinner. But you can also make cute hors d'oeuvres by cutting the finished pizza into small squares with a pizza cutter.

FOR THE DOUGH, place a cutting board on your work surface. In a bowl, mix together the flour, salt, and sugar. Pour ¼ cup of the warm tap water (it should feel body-temperature warm) into a measuring cup. Add the yeast and stir until completely dissolved.

Dump the dry ingredients out onto your cutting board and make a well in the center. Pour the yeast mixture into the well. Add the oil, and then the remaining 1¼ cups water. With a fork, begin pulling the flour into the center to absorb the water. Keep doing this, stirring, until you've incorporated enough flour that the water isn't going to run all over everywhere. Then put the fork aside, and use clean hands to work in the rest of the flour, mashing and kneading until you have a rough dough. Use a pastry scraper (or a spatula) to scrape all the remaining flour off the cutting board and into your dough.

Now knead the dough until it's smooth, supple, and elastic, and no longer sticks to the board or your hands. This will take 10 to 15 minutes. (I like to have my iPod playing.) If, while you're kneading, you find that the dough is a bit dry, add a little water. If it's sticky, add a little flour.

Lightly flour a bowl. Place the dough into it. Use a spray bottle of water to spritz a kitchen towel, and cover the bowl with the damp towel. Set the dough some-place warm, and let it rise until its size has increased by about 1½ times. If your kitchen is nice and warm, this should only take about 1 hour. If your kitchen is cool, it'll take longer, but unless you live in the Arctic, it'll rise eventually.

FOR THE SAUCE, puree the tomatoes through a food mill into a bowl. Add 2 tablespoons of the reserved juice to thin; discard the rest of the juice. Combine the oil, garlic, and peperoncino in a saucepan over low heat and cook until you smell the garlic, but it isn't brown, 1 to 2 minutes. Add the tomato puree, bring to a simmer, and simmer gently, uncovered, for 15 minutes to reduce. Season to taste with a little salt, and add more peperoncino, if you like spicy.

Preheat the oven to 450°F, and arrange a rack in the bottom of the oven. Cut the mozzarella into ½-inch cubes. If you're using fresh mozzarella, put the cubes in a strainer over a bowl and let them drain. (The rectangular mozzarella sold in vacuum-sealed plastic doesn't need to be drained.)

Lightly oil a cookie sheet. When the dough has risen, divide it in half. With clean hands, spread half over the cookie sheet in a round, or rectangle—it makes absolutely no difference. If the dough gives you trouble because it's too elastic, just let it rest for a few minutes and try again. The dough should be thin—it will puff up as it cooks. Use a spoon to spread about half of the sauce over the dough, leaving about ½ inch around the edge sauceless. Bake the pizza for 15 minutes, or until the edges are beginning to go golden, and the dough in the center is no longer wet, then scatter about half of the cheese cubes and basil leaves over the pizza. Return the pizza to the oven and bake until the cheese is melted and the edges of the crust are golden, about 10 more minutes.

While the first pizza is cooking, you can be preparing the second; when the first one comes out, put the second one in the oven.

Cut the pizzas into wedges and serve hot.

THE TWIST

Pizza dough is really pretty easy to make, and I do when I have the time. But when I don't (which is often) I buy the dough readymade. Supermarkets carry it (Whole Foods sells a good one), and I've even bought it from Sbarro, where they'll sell it to you for a couple of dollars.

<figure type="chapter-opener">

CHAPTER THREE

PASTA

</figure>

P asta deserves its own chapter because it is, by far, the most popular food I'm asked to teach. I cook pasta a lot at home, too, because it's very practical for weeknight dining, and I love it. All these recipes can be served in smaller portions as a first course, but it's more likely that you'll be making them as the main event.

My students invariably ask me when they should use fresh pasta instead of dried. In Piacenza, pasta has traditionally meant *fresh* pasta. It's so much a part of the culture that if my grandmother or mom didn't have the time to make it (or, say, it was just too hot to spend the day rolling pasta in the kitchen), they didn't have to look far to buy it; in Italy, entire shops are devoted to selling *pasta fresca*. The stores look just like pastry shops, the glass cases filled with fresh pasta shapes instead of pastry, beautifully laid out, perfectly cut, rolled, and wrapped. When I have the time, I always prefer to make fresh; it's simply the way I grew up. I find it lighter and more delicate than dried. And fresh pasta will absorb the sauce better so that pasta and sauce get amalgamated into a single, delicious *thing*, rather than sauce sitting on top of pasta.

One difference between my generation and my mom's is that, for me, having grown up in America with the dried stuff, fresh pasta is simply a preference, not a rule. Dried pasta is perfectly acceptable. When I'm in a hurry, I use it, and I'm happy to have the option.

Pasta making isn't hard, but there's no question that you'll get better with practice. Start with the easiest shape—tagliatelle—and work your way up to ravioli. When you're a pro, you can tackle the tortelli. Be patient with yourself.

My mom likes to tell the story of her first experience making pasta on her own. She'd done it a zillion times with my grandmother, of course, but Nonna Stella never used recipes. So there's my mom, newly married, making her first batch in her own kitchen. The dough seemed a little bit wet, so she added a little flour. And then it seemed too dry, so she added a little water. Then it was wet again, so a little more flour . . . and on and on, until the dough had grown to this large unworkable mound! Finally, she threw it away and started over. The moral of this story is that even Italians aren't born knowing how to make pasta. It's not a gift. You'll make mistakes, but eventually you'll get it. Don't give up!

All these recipes can be made with fresh or dried pasta, with the exception of the filled shapes and lasagne, which require sheets of fresh pasta. And once you get handy with the five or six basic sauces in this chapter, you can have fun mixing and matching them with pasta shapes, polenta, and gnocchi.

KITCHEN STUFF FOR PASTA

There are only a few pieces of equipment you must have for pasta making: for dried pasta, you'll need a large pot for boiling the pasta, a colander for draining, a skillet or saucepan for the sauce; for fresh pasta, you'll need all those things, plus a pasta machine to roll and cut the pasta dough. (Imperia and Atlas are good brands, available at Amazon.com.) Pasta and sauce can be tossed in a serving bowl, or, if your skillet is large enough, in the skillet in which you made the sauce, and served directly from there. For filled pastas, which should be handled delicately, it's also a good thing to have a large slotted spoon, or even better, one of those wooden-handled spoons with mesh baskets called "spiders" that you can find in Asian stores. Instead of dumping the cooked pasta into the colander in the sink, I set the colander on a plate on the stove and use the spoon to lift the pasta out of the water and into the colander.

BOYARDEE FLASHBACK

The Sauce that's slow-simmered, the old Italian way

The recipe for meat sauce came from my home, Castelnuovo val Tidone. It's thick with tender beef and tangy tomatoes, all spiced just right, then hand-stirred and slowly simmered till the flavor is as smooth as the texture.

But this is only one of my real Italian sauces. Try the meat ball sauce, a delicious, hand-stirred sauce with lean, juicy, all-beef meat balls. Or my mushroom sauce, with mushrooms selected as they were from the grottos of Rome. Or Marinara sauce, a truly distinctive sauce famous in Naples. Use them to top tender spaghetti; or egg, cheese, fish or meat dishes.

As to the compliments on your Italian cooking, let it be our secret that you did it the convenient Chef Boy-Ar-Dee way.

Why chop, chop, simmer and stir? The Chef uses all the fine ingredients you would and handpicks them for freshness.

Chef Boy-Ar-Dee Sauces

For a "hurry-up" dish that's a "fill-'em-up" hit... **Quick** *pure beef*

CHEF BOY-AR-DEE
MEAT BALLS with GRAVY

For other good and hearty meals, ready in minutes, try Chef Boy-Ar-Dee's Spaghetti and Meat Balls, Spaghetti Dinners and Ravioli. All are made with Chef's famous flavor-blended sauce.

You can buy Chef's Spaghetti Sauce with Meat, or Sauce with Mushrooms, separately. Just heat and serve on your favorite dishes. So save time, save money, serve wonderful meals. Make one night a week "Chef Night."

Hurried days mean hurried people. And each day, more and more clever cooks are making Chef Boy-Ar-Dee Meat Balls with Gravy a part of busy-day meals! Comes ready to heat and serve. Wonderful alone or on rice, noodles, potatoes.

In one can, you get 10 top-grade beef meat balls (specially braised to keep in natural juices) and rich brown gravy. Economical, too—about 14¢ a serving!

CHEF BOY-AR-DEE MEAT BALLS with GRAVY

RAVIOLI...
delicious bite-size meat pies

This is Chef Boy-Ar-Dee Ravioli. *Real ravioli* made from an authentic Italian recipe. Tender macaroni pies bursting with beef. Simmered in meaty tomato sauce. Seasoned with the Chef's touch.

So much tastier, easier, quicker and lots thriftier than the frozen kind. Serve Chef Boy-Ar-Dee Ravioli for lunch, supper. For kids, grown-ups.

For meatless meals, try Chef Boy-Ar-Dee Cheese Ravioli. Try Beef Ravioli in the 2-serving or thrifty 5-serving size. Only about 15¢ a serving.

For a hearty, satisfying lunch serve Chef Boy-Ar-Dee Ravioli with a tossed salad.

For a tempting side dish serve Chef Boy-Ar-Dee Ravioli with your favorite meat.

Enjoy instant hors d'oeuvres—you just heat Chef Boy-Ar-Dee Ravioli in a chafing dish.

CHEF BOY-AR-DEE **RAVIOLI**
A meal in a minute with the Chef's touch in it.

Now, ravioli with more beef in every bite!

Watch them go for new Chef Boy-Ar-Dee Ravioli. Bite-size macaroni pies bulging with juicy beef. You still pay the same thrifty price! Still get ravioli seasoned, simmered with the Chef's touch in meaty tomato sauce.

It's so satisfying however you serve it... as a main dish, a side dish or an hors d'oeuvre. Here's the way to get the true taste of Italy. Quicker, easier and thriftier than the frozen kind. Try Chef Boy-Ar-Dee Cheese Ravioli, too.

A meal in a minute with the Chef's touch in it
CHEF BOY-AR-DEE

LEAVING-HOME PENNE RIGATE

WITH BROCCOLI

SERVES 4

	Salt
1½ POUNDS	*broccoli, washed, stems discarded, cut into bite-size florets*
1 POUND	*penne rigate*
¾ CUP	*extra-virgin olive oil*
⅔ CUP	*finely grated pecorino cheese, plus extra for serving*
	Freshly ground pepper

My mom used to make this yummy, Parmesan-and-broccoli-flecked pasta a lot when we were growing up because it was a relatively painless way to get us kids to eat broccoli. And when I went to college, she packed up the recipe for me as part of a set of family recipes that she thought would be easy enough for me to make in my new apartment. This was one of the first dishes I had the courage to cook on my own, and it became a staple of my college years.

But leaving home isn't so easy. I remember the first time I set out to cook this in my new life. It wasn't until I was at the grocery store with recipe in hand that I realized that I couldn't actually *read* it: I never could read my mom's handwriting—I'm forever calling her up to ask her to translate her scrawl. But there I was, first time out, walking up to strangers in the super-market asking, "Can *you* read this?"

These days, my friends have a habit of calling *me* from the supermarket at five P.M., looking for a suggestion for dinner. This is the recipe I give them because it's completely easy and if it's five o'clock and you're still in the supermarket, you can *still* be eating by six fifteen (assuming you don't live too far away).

Note that the broccoli cooks long enough to turn soft and buttery. When you work it all together with your wooden spoon—broccoli, olive oil, and cheese—the broccoli turns into the sauce.

Use a colander with fairly small holes (or a mesh strainer) so that the broccoli buds don't escape into the sink when you drain the pasta.

BRING A BIG POT OF WATER to a boil. Add a good handful of salt (about ¼ cup), enough that you can taste it. Set a fine strainer in the sink.

When the water comes to a boil, add the broccoli and wait until the water returns to a boil. Add the pasta and set the timer to the number of minutes recommended on the box. When the timer rings, drain the penne and broccoli in the colander, then dump them into a large serving bowl. Add the olive oil and mix well with a wooden spoon so that the pasta is coated and the bits of broccoli are well distributed throughout. Add the cheese and stir well until you have a nice, green-speckled sauce. Sprinkle with a little extra cheese, and add some pepper.

FRESH EGG PASTA

MAKES ENOUGH FOR 4 ENTRÉE PLATES

Very early on, before I was old enough to tackle more ambitious kitchen projects, I used to help my mom make fresh pasta. Until I ran into dried pasta in other people's homes, I assumed that fresh was the only kind there was. I spent many childhood hours carefully passing the dough through the pasta machine under my mother's discriminating eye. At Christmastime, we made tons of the stuff.

Some of my students make fresh pasta in a food processor, and I won't argue if you find that easier. We make it the traditional way with a wooden cutting board and pastry scraper. There are fewer dishes to wash, and I can gauge by feel just how much flour the dough needs. But a large bowl will work just fine too. You'll also need a clean kitchen surface—board or counter—to knead the dough.

I can't make fresh pasta without thinking of myself as a skinny ten- or eleven-year-old kid out playing kickball in the neighborhood one day. I overheard one of the neighbors say, "Oh, my God, she's so skinny. . . . Her grandfather must have put her through the spaghetti machine!" Home pasta machines don't actually cut spaghetti, though; they cut only flat noodles: tagliatelle and the very thin angel hair.

THE DOUGH

MAKE A MOUND OF FLOUR on a cutting board or in a large bowl. Make a well in the center of the mound by pushing the flour in the middle out toward the edges. Break the eggs into the center of the well and beat with a fork to break up the eggs. Use the fork to slowly draw the flour from the inside of the well into the center, incorporating the flour into the eggs a little at a time until the mixture is no longer liquid. Put the fork aside, and continue incorporating the flour with clean hands until you have a rough dough. You probably won't use all of the flour—when the dough is no longer sticky, push any excess flour to the edge of the board. (If you're new at this, the flour may have bits of hardened dough in it; in that case, throw it out.) Scrape the board clean with the scraper and dust with a little clean flour. (Or, if you're using a bowl, remove the dough to a clean work surface.) Your hands will be gunky—wash and dry them well.

Knead the dough for 10 minutes, adding a little more clean flour if the dough is sticky, until it is smooth and silky and bounces back when pressed with a finger.

2 CUPS	all-purpose flour, plus extra, if needed
3	large eggs

Bang the ball of dough on the board a couple of times (a mysterious action performed by my inscrutable mother and grandmothers). Wrap it in plastic and set aside in a cool place (no need to refrigerate) for 30 minutes.

ROLLING AND CUTTING PASTA

Once the dough has rested, you're ready to roll it into sheets using a pasta machine. Set up the machine on your kitchen counter and set the rollers on the widest setting. Lay out two clean kitchen towels or a baking sheet dusted with flour on your kitchen counter.

Cut the dough into three pieces. Working with one piece at a time (cover the others with plastic wrap), dust the dough lightly with flour, and roll through the machine to thin it to a sheet. Fold the sheet in half, and roll it through again. Do this once more. The dough should be nice and smooth, with an even color. If you see bits of unincorporated flour or areas of uneven color, fold the dough in half and repeat the rolling process until the dough is smooth. (You can't roll the dough too much at this stage.)

Adjust the machine to the next-thinnest setting, and roll the dough through. Without folding this time, roll the dough through a second time. Adjust to the next thinnest setting. Continue rolling the dough sheet through the machine, twice at each setting, adjusting the machine to make the opening smaller each time. When the sheet gets too long to handle, cut it in half and work with each half separately.

IF YOU'RE MAKING NOODLES, roll the dough until you've reached the next-to-last setting on the machine. Place the dough sheets on the kitchen towels or baking sheets, and let them dry for about 10 minutes. As the first round dries, continue to roll the rest of the dough into sheets the same way, and lay them out to dry. The dough sheets are dry enough when they've developed a plastic-like skin. If the dough is too moist, the pasta will stick together when you cut it into noodles; if it dries too much, it will become brittle and break when you cut it. If you keep making pasta, you're *definitely* going to encounter both problems one day. Don't get frustrated—the only way you're going to learn the correct texture is to blow it a couple of times!

Fit the cutting attachment to the pasta machine and cut the pasta into wide (tagliatelle) or thin (angel hair) noodles. As you cut each sheet into noodles, wrap the noodles loosely around your hand to make a neat "nest," and set the nest back on the towel or baking sheet. If the noodles are at all sticky, toss them with a little flour to keep them from sticking to one another.

IF YOU'RE ROLLING PASTA FOR LASAGNE OR A FILLED PASTA, such as ravioli or tortelli, roll each sheet to the thinnest setting (it should be thin enough to see through). Fill the pasta immediately as described in each recipe while the dough is still a little sticky, so that the doubled sheets will adhere to each other.

UNCLE HECTOR'S TAGLIATELLE
WITH TOMATO SAUCE "IL GIARDINO"

SERVES 4, AS AN ENTRÉE

	UNCLE HECTOR'S TOMATO SAUCE
I (32-OUNCE) CAN	*peeled plum tomatoes, preferably imported Italian*
6 TABLESPOONS	*extra-virgin olive oil, or more, as needed for serving*
I	*onion, chopped*
	Salt and freshly ground pepper
5	*medium fresh basil leaves, cut into strips*
	Fresh Egg Pasta (page 77), or 1 pound dried linguine
¼ TO ⅓ CUP	*finely grated Parmesan cheese*

This is one of the sauces that launched the Chef Boyardee brand.

It helped launch me, too, when I was in the second grade and still new enough to America to be terribly embarrassed by my weird, Italian bag lunches. (While the other kids ate their tuna on Wonder Bread, I nibbled covertly on my Caprese panini, disguised in a napkin.)

I had the part of the fairy godmother in the school play that year. My mom had loaned me one of her wooden spoons—her tomato sauce spoon—to use as a magic wand. "This is a very special spoon, Anna Maria, so take good care of it."

I knew to take her seriously about that spoon. Having grown up with the scarcity of post World War II Italy, she's always been careful with her kitchen tools (she's careful about everything, really); to this day, she uses *one* spoon, only, for her tomato sauce.

On the day of the play, all of us kids were standing backstage, lined up and ready to go on. There was the usual nervous chatter as we waited for the auditorium to fill. The familiar, intoxicating blend of tomato, onion, olive oil, and basil wafted from my "wand."

"Mmm, it smells like Mom's tomato sauce," I murmured to myself, instantly surrounded by comforting memories of dinner and mom and home.

"What are you doing?" A classmate in front of me had caught me in my reverie.

"It's my mom's spoon—it smells like her sauce," I said, handing it over. And pretty soon, there was my mom's "magic" spoon, making its way down the line from kid to kid, their chatter replaced by the sounds of "mmm!" and "oh, wow, this smells so good!"

I was stunned. They liked my food! And it wasn't even dessert! From then on, I had kids asking to trade their lunches for my panini, and everybody wanted to come to dinner at my house.

This recipe makes enough sauce for 1 pound of fresh tagliatelle, or dried linguine, one recipe potato gnocchi (page 54), or one of polenta (page 63). Our recipe uses a 32-ounce can of tomatoes, available at specialty stores. You can get away with a 28-ounce can if you're saucing dried pasta. But fresh pasta absorbs more sauce, so you will need the larger amount; if you can't find the 32-ounce version, use a 28-ounce can and add about half of another 14-ounce can. And if the sauce doesn't thicken well, add a tablespoon of tomato paste.

TO MAKE THE SAUCE, set a food mill over a large bowl. Dump the whole can of tomatoes, with their juices, into the food mill and work the tomatoes though until all that's left in the mill is a handful of dryish tomato pulp and seeds. Discard the pulp and seeds.

Heat the oil in a medium saucepan over low heat. Add the chopped onion and 1 teaspoon salt and cook slowly, stirring every now and then, until the onion is soft and translucent but not brown, 8 to 10 minutes. (Don't let the onion brown, or it may turn the sauce bitter.) Add some pepper and the pureed tomato. Bring the sauce to a boil. Reduce the heat so that the sauce simmers gently. Set the timer for 40 minutes and let the sauce cook, the lid partly ajar, to blend the flavors and thicken. When the timer goes off, add the basil and cook 5 more minutes.

Meanwhile, if you're using fresh pasta, follow the egg pasta recipe on page 77 to make the dough. Let it rest 30 minutes, then follow steps 4 through 8 to cut it into tagliatelle.

When you're ready to eat, bring a large pot of water to a boil. Set a colander in the sink. Add salt to the boiling water until you can taste it (about ¼ cup). Add the fresh or dried pasta, return the water to the boil, and cook until al dente, about 4 minutes for fresh, or follow package instructions for linguine. Drain the pasta in the colander.

THE TWIST

The recipe is typical of the way we make tomato sauce in Piacenza, without garlic. But you may love garlic—lots of my friends and students do—and you should always try to make food taste the way you like. Try adding 1 small clove, chopped, about 2 minutes before the onion finishes cooking (any sooner and you risk burning the garlic).

To serve, dump the pasta into a large pasta bowl. Spoon the sauce on top and toss with a large spoon and fork. Add a little olive oil if the pasta seems dry. Divide the pasta between 4 pasta bowls, or deep plates. Spoon the cheese on top and serve.

RIGATONI

WITH ROASTED TOMATOES

SERVES 4

This is really an Anna recipe: lots of flavor, not tons of work, rather impressive looking, and hard to mess up. If you're intimidated about making a tomato sauce for pasta, this recipe is for you. You don't need a food mill—and, I assure you, anyone can slice a tomato and an onion. Roasted with a little chopped garlic, and Parmesan and pecorino cheeses, the vegetables melt into a luscious muddle that smells divine and tastes just as good.

It's also a terrific summer dish that can be made ahead of time and served at room temperature; taste for seasoning before serving. It works beautifully with any tubular pasta, including penne and penne rigate.

PREHEAT THE OVEN to 400°F and center a rack in the oven.

Spread ¼ cup of the olive oil on a 13-by-17-inch rimmed baking sheet. Scatter the onion slices evenly over the sheet in a single layer. Arrange the tomato slices side by side over the onions so that the entire sheet is evenly covered. Push the slices right up against each other without overlapping them. Sprinkle with about ½ teaspoon salt and ⅛ teaspoon pepper. If using fresh garlic, squeeze it through a press onto the cutting board (not directly onto the tomatoes—you don't want it all to land on one lone tomato). Sprinkle the pressed garlic or garlic salt, if using it, evenly over the tomatoes. Sprinkle the Parmesan so that each tomato slice gets a light covering and then do the same with the pecorino. Drizzle all over with 2 more tablespoons olive oil.

Roast until the edges of the tomatoes are shriveled (some will begin to brown) but the tomato slices themselves have not yet begun to brown, 50 to 60 minutes. (At this point, you can cover the baking sheet with foil and set it aside at room temperature until you're ready to eat; the heat of the just-cooked pasta will rewarm the vegetables.)

For the rigatoni, bring a large pot of water to a boil. Add salt until the water tastes salty (about ¼ cup). Set a colander in the sink. Add the pasta and cook according to the package directions. Drain in the colander. Return the rigatoni to the pot. Scrape in the tomato-onion mixture, add the remaining ¼ cup olive oil, and stir well. Divide it among bowls or plates. Add a little pepper to each, and serve with more Parmesan cheese.

¼ CUP	plus 6 tablespoons extra-virgin olive oil
1	Vidalia (or other sweet) onion, finely sliced
9 TO 10	fresh plum tomatoes sliced into ⅓-inch thick rounds
	Salt and freshly ground pepper
2 CLOVES	garlic, pressed through a garlic press, or ½ teaspoon garlic powder
2½ TABLESPOONS	finely grated Parmesan cheese, plus extra for serving
2½ TABLESPOONS	finely grated pecorino cheese
1 POUND	rigatoni

THE TWIST

I adapted this from my mom's summertime recipe for ripe tomatoes cooked with garlic on top of the stove in olive oil. I figured it would be much easier to cook them in the oven. It is.

PENNE

WITH MUSHROOM SAUCE

SERVES 4

2 CUPS	*water*
1 OUNCE	*dried porcini mushrooms, preferably Italian*
3 TABLESPOONS	*extra-virgin olive oil*
3 TABLESPOONS	*unsalted butter*
1	*medium onion, finely chopped*
1 (32-OUNCE) CAN	*plum tomatoes, preferably Italian, pureed in a food mill*
	Salt and freshly ground pepper
1 POUND	*penne*

When my grandfather and his brothers launched the Chef Boyardee brand, there were just three sauces: the tomato sauce on page 80; a spicy Naples-style tomato sauce; and this mushroom sauce. "Three delightful flavors for a varied menu" was the concept behind the launch. Tomatoes were grown in fields around the factory, and mushrooms were grown inside, with what was then state-of-the-art technology. The mushrooms were harvested daily for the sauce. My dad, who worked at the factory when he was a kid, rotating through the different departments, recalls my grandfather's and Uncle Hector's fastidious attention to those mushrooms, which they personally checked each day before they allowed them to be picked.

My version of Hector's mushroom sauce is made with dried porcini instead of fresh; I love their texture. This is a nice option for a dinner party, in case your guests are vegetarians. If you can't find a 32-ounce can of tomatoes, use one 28-ounce can plus about half of a 14-ounce can.

IN A SMALL SAUCEPAN, bring the water to a boil. Remove it from the heat, add the dried mushrooms, and let stand at least 1 hour, or until the mushrooms are very soft and you feel no hard areas when you press them between your fingers. Set a fine strainer over a bowl. Strain the mushrooms, reserving the soaking liquid. Rinse the mushrooms under cold running water to remove any grit or sand, and drain again. Dry on a paper towel. Chop the mushrooms (you want about ¼-inch pieces) and set aside. Line the strainer with paper towels and set it over a bowl. Strain the mushroom broth into the bowl to remove any grit. You should have about 1 cup broth; set it aside.

Heat the oil and butter in a saucepan over low heat. Add the chopped onion and cook until it is translucent and soft but not brown, 8 to 10 minutes.

Add the tomato puree, the chopped mushrooms, and the strained mushroom broth. Season with ½ teaspoon salt and ¼ teaspoon pepper. Cook, uncovered, at a gentle simmer, stirring occasionally, until the sauce is slightly thickened, about 45 minutes. Taste for seasoning and add more salt and pepper if the sauce needs it.

Bring a large pot of water to a boil for the penne. Add enough salt to the pasta water to make it taste salty (about ¼ cup).

About 10 minutes before the sauce is cooked, put a colander in the sink. Add the penne to the boiling water and cook according to the package directions. Drain in the colander. Dump the pasta into a bowl. Add the sauce and toss with two forks to completely coat the penne with the sauce. Serve immediately.

Uncle Hector inspecting mushrooms at the Milton plant. Quality ingredients were a top priority at the company.

PAGLIA E FIENO

SERVES 4

	Salt
½ POUND	*spaghetti*
½ POUND	*spinach spaghetti*
6 TABLESPOONS	*unsalted butter*
2	*large shallots, chopped small (about ¾ cup)*
1	*slice ham, about ⅓-inch thick (½ pound), cut into ⅓-inch cubes*
1 ¼ CUPS	*heavy cream*
PINCH	*freshly grated nutmeg*
½ CUP	*finely grated Parmesan cheese, plus extra for serving*

The sight of these slender strands of pale green (colored with spinach) and white spaghetti, sauced with a silky mixture of shallots, butter, cream, Parmesan cheese, and bits of baked ham always makes me hungry . . . yum! Paglia e fieno, which means "straw and hay" (for the white and green pasta) was traditionally made around Easter to celebrate the arrival of spinach in the garden. (A roasted spring chicken would also have been on the menu.) I grew up with homemade white and spinach egg pasta, which makes this a particularly light and delicate dish. But I rarely have the time to make two doughs, so I use good-quality dried green and white spaghetti instead. You should too!

BRING A LARGE POT OF WATER TO A BOIL over high heat. Set a colander in the sink.

When the spaghetti water comes to a boil, add enough salt to make the water taste salty (¼ cup), and the white and green spaghetti. Return the water to a boil and cook the spaghetti according to the package directions (about 12 minutes).

Meanwhile, in a large (10- to 12-inch) skillet, melt the butter over low heat. Add the shallots and sprinkle with ½ teaspoon salt. Cook until the shallots are translucent and tender, 8 to 10 minutes. Add the chopped ham, give it a stir, and cook 5 more minutes.

Add the cream to the pan, turn the heat to medium, and let the cream come to a gentle simmer. Simmer until the sauce thickens slightly but isn't gloppy, 3 to 4 minutes. Turn off the heat. Add the nutmeg and the cheese and stir well.

When the spaghetti is cooked, ladle out and reserve about ½ cup of the pasta cooking water. Drain the spaghetti in the colander. Add the spaghetti to the skillet with the sauce and stir gently to coat it with the sauce. Add 2 tablespoons of the pasta water to thin the sauce. Add more if it is still gloppy—the sauce should lightly bathe the spaghetti. Turn the pasta out onto a platter and serve it immediately with extra cheese in a serving bowl.

Burro
prodotto dalla crema
di Latte del
Re dei Formaggi
Peso Netto 125

BOYARDEE FLASHBACK

Due to demand and mass appeal, ads for Chef Boyardee products ran in languages other than English. Here is an example of an ad in Spanish.

Saboree Spaghetti Dinner CHEF BOY-AR-DEE

El paquete lo trae todo
No hay que añadir nada

La salsa es deliciosa y Ud. puede elegir la de carne o la de champiñones. Los spaghetti son tiernos y se cocinan pronto. Y el queso, ya rallado, es de puro sabor Italiano.

Todo esto se obtiene por muy poco dinero.

Goce el verdadero sabor italiano de las cenas de Spaghetti CHEF BOY-AR-DEE

SPAGHETTI AGLIO E OLIO

SERVES 4

Parsley-speckled and garlicky, this spaghetti recipe is just about the simplest, quickest recipe on the planet. The only tricky part is timing: You want the garlic to cook slowly and evenly so that it flavors the oil without browning and is done about the same time as the spaghetti. And if you follow the directions below, this should happen. But you've got to watch the garlic like a hawk—turn your back for an *instant*, and it may overcook.

If reading this makes you so nervous you want to turn the page right now (or if this is your first pasta dish), cook the garlic-oil sauce first and take the pan off the heat. Then cook the spaghetti, rewarm the sauce over medium heat, add the spaghetti, and toss. When you feel more secure, try the other method.

	Salt
4 CLOVES	*garlic*
I POUND	*spaghetti*
IO TO I2 TABLESPOONS	*extra-virgin olive oil, or as needed*
⅛ TEASPOON	*freshly ground black pepper*
⅛ TEASPOON	*peperoncino*
3 TABLESPOONS	*chopped fresh Italian parsley*

BRING A LARGE POT OF WATER TO A BOIL for the pasta and add enough salt to make the water salty (about ¼ cup). Put a colander in the sink.

Meanwhile, chop the garlic as finely as you can.

When the pasta water comes to a boil, add the spaghetti and set the timer to 9 minutes. (If the pasta sticks out of the water, stir with a fork until it softens enough to be completely submerged.)

Measure 10 tablespoons of the oil into an 11-inch skillet and turn the heat to low. Add ¼ teaspoon salt. Add the garlic and cook it very, very gently, watching carefully, until it is tender but not browned, 4 to 5 minutes. Add the black pepper and the red pepper flakes.

By this time, the spaghetti should be cooked. Drain it in the colander, dump it into the skillet with the oil, and toss it with two forks to coat it with the oil. Add the parsley and toss again. If the pasta seems a little dry, add 2 more tablespoons olive oil. Serve right away.

BUCATINI AMATRICIANA

SERVES 4

1 (28-OUNCE) CAN	*peeled plum tomatoes, preferably Italian*
½ POUND	*bacon, preferably thickly sliced and without nitrites*
¼ CUP	*extra-virgin olive oil*
1	*onion, coarsely chopped*
	Salt
⅛ TEASPOON	*peperoncino (see sidebar)*
1 POUND	*bucatini*
¼ CUP	*finely grated pecorino cheese, plus extra for serving*

SHOPPING WITH ANNA

Like black pepper and nutmeg, peperoncino (red pepper flakes) is now sold in those neat, glass bottles with a grinder in the cap. You can grind as you need it, with no additional equipment.

Bucatini is a dried pasta that looks like thick, hollow spaghetti. If you can't find it at your market, use spaghetti (which I like a lot with this sauce). I also like to use mezzi rigatoni here, a completely different shape of pasta that looks like short rigatoni. This is a rustic dish; everything should be roughly chopped.

SET A FOOD MILL OVER A BOWL and purée the tomatoes with their juices; set aside.

Cut each piece of bacon crosswise into 1-inch pieces; set aside.

In an 11-inch skillet, heat the oil over medium-low heat. Add the onion and cook until softened, about 5 minutes. Turn down the heat if you see the onion begin to go golden colored.

Add the bacon pieces, ½ teaspoon salt, and the peperoncino and cook gently without browning until the bacon fat is completely rendered, 12 to 15 minutes. The bacon should look well cooked but neither crisp nor brown.

Add the tomato puree. Bring to a simmer, lower the heat until the tomato simmers very gently, and cook until reduced and thickened, 30 to 35 minutes. Taste for peperoncino, and add more if you like a spicier sauce.

Meanwhile, bring a large pot of water to a boil for the pasta. Add salt until the water tastes salty (about ¼ cup). Put a colander in the sink. When the sauce has cooked 25 minutes, add the pasta to the boiling water and cook according to package directions. Drain in the colander.

Dump the drained pasta into the skillet with the sauce and toss with two forks to coat the pasta with the sauce. Add the cheese and toss well. Serve with more cheese in a bowl on the side.

RIGATONI BOLOGNESE

SERVES 4 (PLUS SAUCE FOR A SECOND MEAL FOR 4)

BOLOGNESE SAUCE	
3 TABLESPOONS	extra-virgin olive oil
3 TABLESPOONS	unsalted butter
I	small onion, chopped as finely as you can (about ¼ cup)
I	small carrot, peeled and chopped as finely as you can (about ¼ cup)
I STALK	celery, the bumpy side peeled with a vegetable peeler, chopped as finely as you can (about ¼ cup)
I POUND	ground beef (85% lean)
1½ TEASPOONS	salt
1¼ CUPS	dry white wine, such as Pinot Grigio
I CUP	milk
⅛ TEASPOON	freshly grated nutmeg
I (35-OUNCE) CAN	tomatoes, pureed in a food mill (you'll need 3½ cups)
	Salt
I POUND	rigatoni
2 TABLESPOONS	extra-virgin olive oil
¼ TO ⅓ CUP	finely grated Parmesan cheese, for serving

The story of how my parents met is something out of an adventure-romance novel. My mother, the heroine, has always been a great traveler. As a young girl, her dream was to become a stewardess so that she could travel the world. When she didn't get the job, she was so distraught, my grandmother said, that she threatened to throw herself out the window. (Believe it.)

Instead, she went to London and then Paris, where she worked as an au pair. In 1968, she was old enough to vote, and decided to return home to to participate in her first election. It was early June, and France was in the middle of the general strike that practically brought down their economy.

She was on the train in the middle of the night, still in France, when the train just stopped. No explanation. No one knew what was happening. It wasn't until daybreak that she and the other passengers could even try to figure out where they were. They walked, en masse, to the nearest village to ask for help. There were no buses running from the village, so she hitchhiked. A Citroën picked her up and took her to the French border, the driver raging all the way at the French students who were ruining his country. From the border, our heroine managed to get a train to Lausanne, Switzerland, and eventually a train to Piacenza. The trip home took forty-eight hours.

She couldn't return to Paris, so she got a job as a guide on the Riviera. When that job ended, she returned to Piacenza.

One day, at the dentist's office, she met a friend who told her that there was an American in town who was looking for someone to speak English with. They met for lunch. According to her story, he struck her as quite a gentleman. My dad is fifteen years older than my mom; his hair was already white then, she says, and he drove a Lincoln Continental, an absurdly large and luxurious car for those days in Italy.

They began dating, and every time they went to dinner, my dad ordered pasta with Bolognese sauce, the creamy, long-cooked meat sauce that's famous in the Emilia-Romagna region. One restaurant in particular, Hotel Roma in Piacenza, was well known for its Bolognese. The waiter would come around to the table with a big pot of the stuff, and ladle it over the spaghetti. My dad loved it. "It was sooooo creamy," my mom, the perfectionist, still sighs. "I always had it in my mind that, since he loved it so much, I wanted to make it like that for him." True love. They married and lived in Piacenza where my brother and I were born until the family moved to the States when I was five.

Never having tasted Hotel Roma's version, I gather that this sauce isn't *quite* as creamy, but you could have fooled me. (And I don't hear my dad complain.) It's pretty delicious. Bolognese sauce is traditionally made with ground beef, cooked very slowly with vegetables, milk, white wine, and tomato, and it's sometimes made with veal, for a lighter sauce. In Piacenza, we don't use garlic, but you may like to.

One 35-ounce can of peeled, Italian tomatoes should yield about 3½ cups puree; or you can use one 28-ounce can plus a 14-ounce can, and refrigerate whatever you don't use for another pasta sauce.

IN A LARGE, DEEP POT OR DUTCH OVEN, heat the oil and butter over medium-low heat. Add the onion and cook 2 minutes. Add the carrot and celery and stir well with a wooden spoon. Cook until the vegetables are softened but not browned, about 5 more minutes. Add the meat and break it into small bits with the spoon. Add the salt and stir. Set the timer for 12 minutes and cook, continuing to break the meat into bits, until the meat is no longer pink, but not browned.

Add the wine. Set the timer for 20 minutes. Adjust the heat, and simmer gently until the wine has completely reduced. You should hear the oil sizzle again.

Add the milk and the nutmeg. Continue simmering gently until the milk has almost completely evaporated and you hear the oil sizzle again, 12 to 15 minutes.

Add the tomato purée, and return the sauce to a very low simmer. Partially cover and simmer on the lowest possible heat for 3 hours. Check the sauce once in a while to make sure it's not cooking too fast. When it's done, reserve half to serve immediately. Cover and refrigerate or freeze the other half for another day.

Bring a large pot of water to a boil and add enough salt to make it taste salty (about ¼ cup). Place a colander in the sink. Add the rigatoni to the boiling water and cook according to the package instructions. Drain in the colander.

Meanwhile, return the reserved sauce to a simmer. Put the rigatoni in a large serving bowl. Add the hot Bolognese sauce and the oil. Toss well. Sprinkle with cheese and serve.

LASAGNE

SERVES 8 TO 10

This is the authentic recipe as we make it in Piacenza and in the region of Emilia Romagna, where the dish originated. It's *almost* the authentic recipe, I should say; in Emilia Romagna, it is made with fresh green pasta (colored with spinach). But there are enough steps to this recipe without making green pasta, so we stick to regular egg pasta.

This recipe is probably different than you're used to. It's made with thin sheets of fresh pasta layered with Bolognese meat sauce, a béchamel sauce (called *besciamella* in Italian), and grated Parmesan cheese. (Versions with ricotta and mozzarella cheeses are typical of southern Italy.) It's light and delicate. And though the besciamella makes it rich and luscious, it's still less saucy than Americans are used to. Italians don't use a lot of sauce; as with all pasta dishes, lasagne is about the pasta as much as the sauce. Homemade pasta is so delicious, I think you'll fall in love with this version, whatever your taste.

It's also a full day's work. (I know this from long experience: my mom and I used to make individual, mini lasagne for all of our friends at Christmastime.) I strongly recommend *not* doing it all in one day; you'll run screaming from the kitchen and never make it again. (You may never *cook* again. Period.) So take it easy on yourself. Make the Bolognese sauce at least a day (or several) in advance. You can make the besciamella and the pasta on the day you plan to assemble the lasagna. Bake it right after you assemble it, or refrigerate it and bake it the next day, or even two days later.

For vegetarians, the mushroom sauce on page 84 works very well in place of the Bolognese.

FOLLOW THE RECIPE FOR FRESH EGG PASTA (page 77) to make the pasta dough. (The quantities are different, but the process is exactly the same.) Wrap it in plastic and let rest at room for temperature 30 minutes while you make the besciamella sauce.

FOR THE BESCIAMELLA, in a saucepan, melt the butter over medium heat and cook until it bubbles. Remove the pan from the heat. Add the flour and stir well with a wooden spoon to blend; there should be almost no lumps. Return the pan to the heat and stir until completely smooth. Let the mixture bubble for 2 minutes, stirring constantly, and making sure to get into the sides

	Fresh Egg Pasta (page 77), made with 1⅓ cups flour and 2 eggs

BESCIAMELLA

6 TABLESPOONS	unsalted butter, plus extra for dotting the top
4½ TABLESPOONS	all-purpose flour
3 CUPS	milk, plus extra for thinning
¼ TEASPOON	salt
⅛ TEASPOON	freshly grated nutmeg
2 TABLESPOONS	finely grated Parmesan cheese
1	recipe Bolognese Sauce (page 92)
	Salt
1 TABLESPOON	extra-virgin olive oil for cooking the pasta
6 TO 8 TABLESPOONS	finely grated Parmesan cheese
1 TABLESPOON	unsalted butter, cut into bits

KITCHEN STUFF

The only practical way to get the cooked sheets of pasta out of the pot and into the colander is a wire-meshed spider, available at Asian cooking supply stores. A slotted spoon will not *work, nor will tongs.*

of the pan. Add the milk, gradually at first and stirring constantly, until blended, and the rest more quickly. Cook without simmering, stirring constantly, until the sauce has thickened, 8 to 10 minutes. Remove the pan from the heat. Add the salt, nutmeg, and cheese and stir until smooth. Dot the top all over with bits of butter to keep a skin from forming. Set the sauce aside.

Bring a large pot of water to a boil for the pasta. Add enough salt to make the water taste salty (about ¼ cup) and add the olive oil. Set a colander in a baking pan close to your work station. Get together six kitchen towels and spread three of them on a clean work space. Butter a 9-by-13-inch baking dish.

THE TWIST

The way my mom taught me to make lasagne was the way her mom taught her: We roll, cook, and cut the pasta as we layer the lasagne. That's great if there are two of you, but if you are on your own, it's much easier to roll and cook all the pasta at once, and cover it with kitchen towels to keep it from drying out while you assemble the dish. (Unless your towels are very large, you will need six of them.)

Attach the pasta machine to a kitchen counter and set the rollers to the widest setting. Cut off about one-third of the dough; cover the rest with plastic. Follow steps 4 through 6 and step 9 to roll the dough to the thinnest setting. Place the dough sheet on a cutting board. Cut it into lengths about the length of the baking dish. (No need to be precise; the dough will expand as it cooks, and you'll cut and piece as needed.)

Add the pasta sheets to the boiling water and set the timer for 2 minutes. When the timer goes off, remove the pasta sheets from the water with a spider and put them in the colander to drain; set the colander in the sink and run cold water over it until it is cool enough to handle. Spread flat in a single layer on one of the kitchen towels. Cover with another towel. Repeat to roll, cut, and cook the rest of the pasta, spreading the sheets on the towels, and covering them with two more towels.

Spread the bottom of the buttered baking dish with a thin, even layer of the Bolognese sauce (use about a quarter of the sauce).

Arrange two of the pasta sheets over the sauce, overlapping them along the center line. If the sheets are a couple of inches too long, just fold over the edges. If they're a teeny bit too short, no problem; cut and piece in some more pasta to fit.

Arrange two more pasta sheets over the first layers, piecing as needed. (This first layer of pasta is doubled—four sheets in all. From now on, the pasta layers will be single layers using only two sheets each.)

Spread the pasta with another thin, even layer of Bolognese sauce (use another quarter of the total amount of sauce). You'll be able to see the pasta through the sauce. Add about one quarter of the besciamella, spooning it on in blobs and gently smoothing with the spoon. It won't cover the Bolognese sauce evenly at all—it will stay in blobs that are sort of connected to one another. Sprinkle 1½ to 2 tablespoons of the Parmesan cheese over the besciamella.

Layer two more sheets of pasta over the besciamella, overlapping along the centerline. Spread with another thin layer of Bolognese sauce (this is the third quarter), and then spoon another quarter of the besciamella on top. Sprinkle with 1½ to 2 more tablespoons Parmesan.

Use two more sheets of pasta to make a third layer of pasta, overlapping along the centerline. Spread with the rest of the Bolognese and then another quarter of the besciamella. Sprinkle on another 1½ to 2 tablespoons Parmesan.

Layer two more sheets of pasta on top. (This is all the pasta you'll need; if you have some left over, cut it into pieces and warm it up with melted butter and Parmesan cheese for lunch.) The besciamella will probably have thickened up quite a bit by this time; if so, add a little milk to thin it. Then spread the rest of the besciamella evenly over the pasta to cover. Sprinkle with the remaining 1½ to 2 tablespoons Parmesan, and dot the top all over with the tablespoon of butter.

Preheat the oven to 375°F. Bake the lasagne until it is bubbling and a light, golden crust forms on the top, 35 to 45 minutes. Remove it from the oven and let it stand, covered with foil, about 10 minutes to firm up before cutting.

SQUASH RAVIOLI

WITH BUTTER AND SAGE

MAKES 85 TO 90 RAVIOLI

	FILLING
1 CUP (8 OUNCES)	*whole-milk ricotta cheese*
1 (20-OUNCE) PACKAGE	*cubed, peeled, and seeded butternut squash*
1½ TEASPOONS	*salt*
¾ CUP	*finely grated Parmesan cheese*
1	*large egg yolk*
½ TEASPOON	*freshly ground pepper*
⅛ TEASPOON	*freshly ground nutmeg*
	Fresh Egg Pasta (page 77), with 2 teaspoons milk added along with the eggs
	SAGE BUTTER
7 TABLESPOONS	*unsalted butter*
7	*large fresh sage leaves*
5 TABLESPOONS	*finely grated Parmesan cheese*
	Freshly ground pepper, if you like
	KITCHEN STUFF
	Ravioli form
	Rolling pin
	A slotted spoon or wire-meshed spider
	Fluted pastry cutter

Squash and pasta are two of my favorite foods; put them together in one dish, and I'm in heaven!

These ravioli are traditional to Piacenza, to the entire region of Emilia-Romagna, in fact, because squash, called *zucca*, is plentiful throughout the region. I love the mild sweetness of the squash, particularly in combination with the delicate pasta.

Last fall, when we were in Milan on business, I talked Jack into taking a train to Piacenza for lunch to indulge my passion for these ravioli. Jack is a longtime fan of my spinach-ricotta ravioli (made exactly like these, but filled with the spinach-ricotta stuffing on page 102), and I wasn't sure he'd go for the squash. But he's also the type who needs to taste *everything*, particularly if we're traveling someplace known for its local cuisine. (He'll call the waiter over after dinner and say, "So . . . what's good?" And we'll have to try it.) I had a plate of the squash, he had the ricotta-spinach ravioli, and we got a plate of tortelli for good measure. We demolished all three, and agreed that lunch was definitely worth the hour on the train.

In Italy, these ravioli are a fall-through-winter dish. In America, they're perfect for Thanksgiving. If, like any thrifty Italian housewife, you use all the scraps, this recipe should make just under ninety 2-inch ravioli. Which *should* feed 6 to 8 people.

However.

I recently ran a test on Jack and myself to confirm the yield. I cooked thirty ravioli: ten for me and twenty for him. I figured he couldn't possibly get through that many. But he did. And he would have gone for more. So figure the recipe will serve between four and eight, depending on the enthusiasm of your diners. And remember that your guests may eat more than usual if they're not used to the delicacy of homemade ravioli.

FOR THE FILLING, line a fine strainer with a double layer of paper towels and set the strainer over a bowl. Scrape the ricotta into the strainer and set aside at least 1 hour, or refrigerate overnight, to drain.

Preheat the oven to 400°F. Place the squash cubes on a small, unoiled baking sheet. Sprinkle with 1 teaspoon of the salt and toss well. Cover loosely with foil and bake until the squash is very soft, about 40 minutes. Let cool.

While the squash cooks, follow steps 1 through 4 of the recipe for Fresh Egg Pasta on page 77 to make the pasta dough, adding the milk with the eggs. Wrap the dough in plastic and let rest at room temperature 30 minutes while you finish the filling.

When the squash has cooled, mash it in a large bowl with a potato masher or press it through a ricer, until it is very smooth. (You should have almost 1 cup puree.) Stir in the drained ricotta cheese. Add the Parmesan, the egg yolk, the remaining ½ teaspoon salt, the pepper, and the nutmeg. Stir until the mixture is completely blended.

Set up the pasta machine and turn the rollers to the widest setting. Set a 9-by-13-inch baking dish or a rimmed baking sheet on your kitchen counter; sprinkle with a little flour. Dust the ravioli form with flour, too.

Cut off about one third of the pasta dough; rewrap the rest and set it aside. Dust the dough lightly with flour, and roll it through the machine as described in steps 5 and 6 of the recipe on page 78. When you get to the thinnest setting, roll the dough only *once*—otherwise, it will get too thin.

Place the dough sheet over the ravioli form. It should be wide enough to cover two rows of eight; it will probably be too long—don't worry about that, you'll use that part later. Use a spoon to fill each ravioli indentation with about ¾ teaspoon filling. Roll another dough sheet to the thinnest setting and place it over the filled pasta. Roll a rolling pin over the form a couple of times until the metal edges poke through the dough. Remove the whole line of filled ravioli (it will hold together in one sheet) and flip it over onto your work surface so that the rounded sides of the ravioli are on top. Cut between each ravioli with a fluted pastry cutter. Press together any edges that are not well sealed, and place the ravioli in a single layer in the baking dish or on the baking sheet.

You should have a few inches of doubled dough scraps left over; separate the layers and lay one piece over as many of the ravioli forms as will fit. Fill, cover, and cut into ravioli. You may need to do this a couple of times to use all the scraps that are wide enough. Discard any bits of dough that are too small or too thin.

Although you can make ravioli without one, I wouldn't dream of tackling this pasta without a ravioli form, a rectangular piece of equipment with square or round shapes marked off with raised metal edges and indented in the centers. A rolling pin is equally essential. You place a sheet of pasta over the form, spoon a little filling into each ravioli, cover with another sheet of pasta, and roll the pin over the form to stick the pasta sheets together. The rolling pin does all the work. Forms for 2-inch ravioli, by Imperia (model number 570-12), are available at Amazon.com. A slotted spoon or wire-meshed spider is also helpful.

Continue rolling and filling the dough. When you complete one layer of ravioli in the baking dish or baking sheet, cover it with a sheet of freezer paper, parchment, or waxed paper, sprinkle on a little flour, and make another layer. (To freeze the ravioli, just cover the baking dish and place it in the freezer. When the ravioli are frozen solid, remove them to a resealable plastic bag and return them to the freezer.)

If you're going to eat the ravioli immediately, bring a large pot of water to a boil. Add enough salt to make the water taste salty (about ¼ cup). Set a colander in a baking dish next to the stove.

FOR THE SAGE BUTTER, melt the butter with the sage leaves in a small saucepan over low heat and let the butter bubble 2 to 3 minutes without browning. Remove from the heat.

Add half of the ravioli to the boiling water. Once the water returns to a simmer (just a *simmer*—if it boils too hard, the ravioli will fall apart), set the timer to 3 minutes. When the timer buzzes, remove one ravioli with a slotted spoon or spider and taste it. If it is tender, carefully transfer all the ravioli to the colander. If not, cook 1 to 2 more minutes, then drain. Return the water to a boil and cook and drain the rest of the ravioli the same way.

Rewarm the sage butter. Spoon some of it over the bottom of a serving platter large enough to hold the ravioli comfortably. Sprinkle with about 1 tablespoon of the grated cheese. Spoon the drained ravioli onto the platter. Spoon over the rest of the melted butter, and the sage leaves (they're good to eat). Sprinkle with the remaining 4 tablespoons cheese. Sprinkle with pepper, if you want to.

LADIES' HOME JOURNAL

"Enjoy Ravioli as truly Italian as the Tower of Pisa"

This very evening—at home—you can sit down to ravioli as it's made to delight Italians themselves... as it's served here in Pisa, for instance.

Your first taste of Chef Boy-Ar-Dee Ravioli lets you know *this* is the true Italian dish . . .

Miniature macaroni pies tender as butter, shaped just-so, filled with pure ground beef . . . then simmered for hours in a special sauce made from juicy red tomatoes, beef and rich beef stock. All nicely spiced with Chef's incomparable Italian touch.

Delicious idea for family supper or a hearty "company" snack—and so quick! Chef Boy-Ar-Dee Ravioli comes ready to heat. In two- or five-serving cans . . . only about 14¢ a serving. Enjoy Italian cooking at its irresistible best!

CHEF BOY-AR-DEE®
real Italian-style Ravioli

Although it was not part of the original line of products, ravioli was soon added and quickly became a favorite among consumers.

TORTELLI PIACENTINI

SERVES 6, AS AN ENTRÉE

FILLING

I POUND	*whole-milk ricotta cheese*
5 OUNCES	*spinach (not baby spinach)*
	Salt and freshly ground pepper
I	*large egg*
PINCH	*freshly ground nutmeg*
I CUP	*finely grated Parmesan cheese, plus more for serving*
	Fresh Egg Pasta (page 77), made with 2½ cups flour and 4 eggs

NUTTY SAGE BUTTER

2 STICKS (I CUP)	*unsalted butter*
6 LEAVES	*fresh sage*

KITCHEN STUFF

	A slotted spoon or wire-meshed spider

Many Sunday mornings, I'd follow my mother into the kitchen to help make these delicious little pastas stuffed with a filling made with spinach, ricotta, and Parmesan cheeses. Tortelli are a specialty of Piacenza, and they're still so unique to that area that you're unlikely to find them elsewhere.

Before any food touched her hands, my mother would slip off her rings and bundle them together with one of those green twisty ties—the kind you get at the supermarket to tie up your bags of produce. The rings would go on the windowsill for safekeeping. And we'd begin to make the dough.

My mother has beautiful hands. They're strong and capable and particularly adept at the delicate work of stuffing and folding tortelli (even after many years of practice, mine still look clumsy next to hers). She also wears gorgeous rings, the kind a little girl couldn't help but admire. Those glamorous objects tied up in a plain, supermarket twist-tie were the essence of my elegant and down-to-earth mother. And of these homey-but-incredibly-delicate tortelli.

The pasta for tortelli—for any stuffed pasta, in fact—is rolled to the thinnest setting on the pasta machine so that even when the pasta is folded and doubled, it's not too thick. You'll end up with trimmings from cutting the rolled pasta strips into squares. Pretend to be Italian: save the scraps, let them air-dry until they form a plasticky skin, and then cut them into tagliatelle to sauce with whatever you've got on hand.

In case it's not obvious, tortelli are *not* Monday night food. They're more like a Sunday-afternoon project. Ask a friend to help.

FOR THE FILLING, line a fine strainer with a double layer of paper towels and place the strainer over a bowl. Scrape the ricotta into the strainer and set aside at least 1 hour, or cover and refrigerate overnight, to drain.

Follow steps 1 through 3 of the recipe for Fresh Egg Pasta on page 77 to make the pasta dough. (The quantities are different, because you need a little more dough, but the process is exactly the same.) Cover with plastic wrap and set aside to rest for 30 minutes while you make the filling.

Tear the stems off the spinach and wash the leaves well. Spin them in a salad spinner. Place a fine strainer in the sink. Put the spinach into a medium

saucepan with just the water that still clings to the leaves and a pinch of salt. Cover the saucepan and set it over low heat. Cook until the spinach is wilted, about 5 minutes. A lot of green liquid will have accumulated in the pan with the spinach; dump everything through the fine strainer and drain well, using a fork to press out as much liquid as possible. Once the spinach is very dry, place it on a cutting board and chop it finely with a large knife.

Spoon the drained ricotta into a mixing bowl. Add ¼ teaspoon salt, ¼ teaspoon pepper, the egg, and the nutmeg and stir with a fork to blend. Stir in the Parmesan, and then the chopped spinach until completely blended.

Set up your pasta machine on the kitchen counter and set the rollers on the widest setting. Lay out two clean kitchen towels, or a baking sheet sprinkled with a little flour.

Follow steps 4 through 6 and step 9 of the recipe for Fresh Egg Pasta on page 78 to roll out the pasta dough, dividing the dough into quarters as you begin rolling, rather than into thirds.

Place a finished dough sheet on your floured work surface. If your sheet is skinny, you'll get one, long 2½-inch-wide strip from it: use a ruler, and trim top and bottom edges to cut it to size. (If your sheet is wider, you may be able to squeeze out two strips.) Cut the strips into 2½-inch squares. Reserve the trimmings.

To fill the tortelli, pick up one of the squares and smear a generous ½ teaspoon of filling over the center. Then turn the dough square so that it looks like a diamond, with points at the top and bottom. Starting at the bottom left, fold in the outside edge and press to seal. Fold in the opposing bottom edge; this time, pinch between thumb and forefinger to seal. Then back to the first side, fold, and pinch. Continue doing this, alternating sides, until the entire length of the pasta has been folded into something that looks like a braid and the filling is entirely enclosed. Pinch the top to seal in the filling.

Place the tortelli in a single layer on the baking sheet or kitchen towels. Continue to roll and fill all the tortelli. When your baking sheet is full, cover the tortelli with a sheet of waxed paper or parchment paper and make another layer. (To freeze the tortelli, cover the baking sheet and place it in the freezer. When the tortelli are frozen solid, remove them to a resealable plastic bag and return them to the freezer.)

To cook the pasta, bring a large pot of water to a boil. Add enough salt that the water tastes salty (about ¼ cup). Set a colander on a plate near the stove.

When the water comes to a boil, add half of the tortelli. When they rise to the surface, set a kitchen timer to 2 minutes. When the timer buzzes, transfer the tortelli to the colander with a spider or a slotted spoon. Cook and drain the rest of the tortelli the same way.

FOR THE NUTTY SAGE BUTTER, melt the butter with the sage leaves in a small saucepan over medium-low heat until the butter turns a golden brown color and smells nutty, 3 to 4 minutes. Take the pan off the heat.

To serve, spoon the tortelli into shallow bowls. Spoon the butter and sage leaves over the top. Sprinkle with more Parmesan, if you like (Jack doesn't, I do).

THE TWIST

In Italy, we use sheep's milk ricotta in lot of dishes, especially in mixtures for filled pastas (like tortelli and butternut ravioli) and to make chicchi. The cow's milk ricotta available in America is looser and more watery than what we're used to. That's why, to adapt the recipes, we drain the cow's milk ricotta for at least an hour, and preferably overnight.

ANOLINI IN BRODO

SERVES 6 (MAKES ABOUT 120 ANOLINI)

This is a *very* traditional pasta from Piacenza, typically served at Christmastime when the women in families throughout the town wake up early to roll and fill the anolini for Christmas lunch. Anolini (also spelled agnolini—it means "belly buttons") are served with the broth from bollito misto (page 135). They are made two different ways: very small, to serve in a cup of broth as soup (oh, my gosh, what a lot of work!), or larger (as in this recipe), to serve in a bowl of broth as a primo. I definitely serve them as an entrée.

If you don't have *real* broth on hand, canned chicken broth is a nice, quick substitute. Or you can cook the anolini in boiling salted water and serve them with the cream sauce on page 86.

For each sheet of pasta that you roll and fill, you'll end up with a bunch of trimmings. Don't throw them away! That's dinner. Cook the scraps in a pot of boiling water and toss them with mushroom sauce (page 84), tomato sauce (page 80), sage butter and Parmesan (page 98), or plain old melted butter and grated cheese.

Anolini freeze well. If you're serving two people, plan for 1½ cups broth and 20 anolini per person, and freeze the rest for another night. It's best if you make the filling the day before you plan to stuff the anolini. An overnight in the fridge gives all the flavors a chance to meld.

FOR THE FILLING, make two shallow cuts in the beef with a small knife and insert a garlic slice into each cut. Heat the oil in a small, heavy-bottomed saucepan over medium heat until it sizzles. Add the meat and cook, turning once, until nicely browned on both sides, 4 to 6 minutes each side. Sprinkle with ¼ teaspoon salt and ⅛ teaspoon pepper. Add the wine, and cook until it has almost completely evaporated. Cover, adjust the heat to the lowest possible setting, and cook until the meat is very tender, 2 to 2½ hours. Check the meat every now and then; if the bottom of the pan begins to brown too much, add a little water. But mostly you want the meat to be cooking very slowly in its own juices.

Remove the cooked meat to a cutting board. There should be some juices and fat left in the pan. Add the bread crumbs and stir with a spoon, particularly into

	FILLING
ONE (7-OUNCE) PIECE	beef chuck
½ GARLIC CLOVE	cut into 2 slices
1 TABLESPOON	extra-virgin olive oil
	Salt and freshly ground pepper
¼ CUP	dry white wine, such as Pinot Grigio
1 SMALL (ABOUT 3-INCH) SPRIG	fresh rosemary
2 TABLESPOONS	dried bread crumbs, or as needed
1	large egg
PINCH	freshly ground nutmeg
1½ CUPS	finely grated Parmesan cheese
	Fresh Egg Pasta (page 77), made with 1½ cups flour and 3 eggs
10 CUPS (ABOUT)	broth from 1 recipe Bollito Misto (page 135), or 10 cups canned low-sodium chicken broth
	Finely grated Parmesan cheese, for serving

the corners, to soak up all the juices. (If the mixture is soupy, add more bread crumbs.) Scrape the bread crumbs out into a bowl.

Cut the meat into chunks and put them in a food processor. Process until very finely chopped. This will take a couple of minutes—process for about 20 seconds and then take off the lid and taste the meat; continue processing until the meat is very soft, but don't let it become a paste. Scrape it into the bowl with the bread crumbs. Break the egg into another small bowl. Add ⅛ teaspoon salt, ⅛ teaspoon pepper, and the nutmeg, and beat with a fork to combine. Pour into the bowl with the meat and stir with the fork to blend. Add the cheese and knead with clean hands until all ingredients are well combined. Cover and refrigerate overnight, if possible.

Follow steps 1 through 3 in the recipe for Fresh Egg Pasta on page 77 to make the pasta dough. Wrap it in plastic and let it rest 30 minutes.

Attach a pasta machine to a kitchen counter and turn the rollers to the widest setting. Lightly flour your work surface. Line a 9-by-13-inch baking dish with a piece of parchment paper and dust with flour. Cut off a small piece of dough; cover the rest with a piece of plastic wrap while you work. Dust the dough lightly with flour and roll it through the machine to the thinnest setting, as described in steps 4 through 6 and step 9 on page 78 of the egg pasta recipe. Place the finished dough sheet on your floured work surface and use a fluted pastry cutter to cut a 2-inch-wide strip. Cut the strip crosswise to make 2-inch squares.

To shape the anolini, position one of the pasta squares in front of you, like a diamond, with one point facing up. Pinch off a small piece of the filling (a little less than ½ teaspoon) and center it in the pasta diamond. Fold the top half over the filling and match up the sides to make a triangle with a lump of filling in the center. Press all around the filling with the index finger of each hand to flatten and seal the dough. Press firmly—you want to compress and thin the overlapping layers of dough so that the anolini aren't tough. Take hold of both "arms" of the triangle between thumb and index finger of each hand, and lift up gently so that the top point stays on the work surface, and you make a crease between the filling and the top of the triangle. Set one index finger upright on the work surface, touching the pasta in the center of the triangle between the two "arms." Then wrap the arms around your finger to meet. Press the ends of the arms firmly together to seal, and firmly compress the dough to the thickness of a single layer. Place in the parchment-lined baking dish. Continue on in this way to roll and fill all the anolini, arranging them in the baking dish in a single layer. When the dish is full, lay a sheet of parchment paper on top, lightly flour it, and continue layering until you've used all the dough (you may have a little of the filling left over). At this point, you can freeze the anolini for another day and collapse in exhaustion. (When they're frozen, dump the anolini into a resealable plastic bag.) Or . . .

To serve, bring the broth to a simmer in two saucepans, half in each saucepan. (If you're using the broth from bollito and you come up a little short of 10 cups, add canned broth to make up the difference.) Add 60 anolini to each pan, return the broth to a simmer, set the timer, and cook 3 minutes. Remove the pans from the heat, cover, and let stand 2 minutes. Divide the anolini among six pasta bowls using a slotted spoon, and pour the broth over. Sprinkle each serving with a little more Parmesan cheese.

THE TWIST

This meat stuffing is a terrific filling for stuffed pastas, and it's just as nice in ravioli, which are much less work to make than anolini. Roll and fill the ravioli just like you make the squash ravioli on page 98.

SEAFOOD, POULTRY, AND MEATS

These are the entrée dishes (*secondi*, in Italian) I grew up with. These days, my diet consists mostly of pasta, chicken, and vegetable dishes—in part by predilection, in part because they're quick and contemporary—so I reserve many of the recipes in this chapter for special-occasion cooking.

I recommend the branzino, a whole fish, steamed in the oven under a blanket of coarse salt, for a small dinner party. It's an unusual entrée, delicious and light, that requires surprisingly little work but will make you look like a whiz in the kitchen.

Shrimp Limoncello, whole or chopped, makes an eye-catching topping for bruschetta at cocktail parties. Chicken and veal cutlets are simple, everyday dishes that work particularly well in a buffet. I like my grandmother's Polenta Pasticciata for large parties, because, like lasagne, it can be made well in advance and reheated at the last moment (in fact, it's better that way). And capon, served with a mushroom-sausage bread stuffing, is my favorite choice for Thanksgiving or Christmas dinner.

Veal is extremely popular in Italy and easy to find there. Less so here. There are three veal recipes in this chapter and all of them can be made with another meat: chicken cutlets work fine for veal cutlets, a fat pork chop makes a nice substitute for a veal chop, and a pork shoulder roast will serve in place of the veal roast.

BRANZINO BAKED UNDER A SALT CRUST

SERVES 1 TO 2

1	*very fresh branzino with head and tail, gutted, but unscaled (about 1 pound)*
3½ TO 4 CUPS	*coarse salt*
1 (4-INCH) SPRIG	*fresh rosemary*
1 CLOVE	*garlic, cut into 5 thin slices*
	Extra-virgin olive oil, for drizzling
	Lemon wedges, for serving

SHOPPING WITH ANNA

You really need a fish market that you trust for this dish because you want the fish to be very fresh. I don't want to give the impression that you'd ever want anything but very fresh fish, but with this preparation, there will be nothing to disguise the taste. You can tell a fresh fish by the way it looks (bright and shiny and plump) and smells (briny and pleasant).

The first time I ever met a whole fish face-to-face on my plate was in Sardinia. I was thirteen years old and visiting my best friend, Paola, whose father loves to fish. He'd catch a whole bunch of smallish fish called orata (a little smaller than the branzino in this recipe) and throw them on the grill. At dinner, everyone got his or her own fish. I was, like, "Oh, my God, what do I do with *this*?"

It turned out that eating a whole fish wasn't so hard—and they're surprisingly easy to cook.

I got this recipe for whole branzino cooked under a salt crust from my good friend Lorenzo Uras, who is also from Sardinia. Branzino is a smallish, narrow variety of European sea bass. I stuff the belly with garlic and rosemary, tuck the fish under a thick blanket of coarse salt, and bake. The salt hardens to a crust that's easy to crack open, and the fish is so moist and flavorful, it needs only a drizzle of olive oil and squeeze of lemon to finish it. It's perfect for two, with spinach (page 162) and roasted potatoes (page 157) or butternut squash (page 160).

I always teach this recipe because it's so hard to mess up; the salt crust gently steams the fish, so it absolutely will not be dry. It's also a great example of something that *seems* difficult but is really simple; in fact, this may be the easiest recipe in the book. And people are always impressed.

With a larger pan and double the salt, it's easy to cook two fish; the timing is exactly the same.

PREHEAT THE OVEN to 400°F. Rinse the fish well under cold running water, especially in the belly cavity, to remove any traces of blood. Dry well inside and out with paper towels.

Cover the bottom of a 10- by 12-inch aluminum pan with about ¼ inch salt; you'll need about 1½ cups. Arrange the fish diagonally in the pan over the salt. Open the belly cavity and lay the rosemary branch, lengthwise, in the cavity. Line up the garlic slices, side by side, on top of the rosemary. Press the edges of the cavity together to protect the flesh from the salt. Then pour salt over the fish to completely cover it, except for the head and tail. (You'll need about 2 cups more salt.) Put some water in a bowl, dip your fingers into it, and sprinkle

a little water over the top layer of salt; you'll use about 2 teaspoons. This will help to create the crust.

Bake the fish until the eye turns white and opaque, exactly 40 minutes. Remove the pan from the oven and let sit for a couple of minutes.

Use the rounded end of a regular dinner knife to crack the top layer of salt. Push the crust off the fish in chunks. Using a fork and knife, lift the fish onto a clean plate with the opening of the belly cavity facing you. With the same knife, cut off the tail; discard. Starting at the belly opening, insert the knife between skin and flesh, wherever you can get the knife in. Then lift off the skin (it should come off in one large piece or a couple of smaller pieces). Cut down the dark line that runs along the top fillet from the head all the way to the tail and divides the fillet in half. The flesh will separate easily at that line. Use the fork and knife to push the fish off the bone, on either side of that center line. Lift the fillet in pieces off the bone and onto a plate, removing any gelatinous or dark-colored bits. When you've entirely removed the top fillet, discard the rosemary and garlic. Lift up the backbone at the tail and lift the bones and head off the plate; discard. Then cut the bottom fillet in half along the center line, push the flesh off the skin, and lift the pieces onto the plate.

Drizzle with olive oil and serve with lemon wedges.

SHRIMP LIMONCELLO

SERVES 2

Like the branzino on page 112, this dish also comes from Sardinia (and was also donated by my friend Lorenzo Uras), where they make the sweet, lemony liqueur called limoncello. This recipe is all about lemon—the grated zest adds a bright, sharp tang to balance the sweetness of the liqueur. The garlic adds a nice savory undertone.

Shrimp limoncello served with rice make a quick, elegant dinner for two. But more often, I serve the shrimp as antipasto: remove the tails and place one whole shrimp on a bruschetta, or chop and spoon it onto crackers. It's a very cute mouthful.

WASH THE SHRIMP UNDER COLD running water and pat dry completely on paper towels. Line a plate with paper towels and set it near the stove.

In a 12-inch skillet, preferably nonstick, combine the oil, garlic, and onion, if using, over low heat. Cook the garlic without allowing it to color (really, what you're doing is flavoring the oil), 30 to 60 seconds. Add the shrimp in a single layer and cook 3 minutes. Turn, and cook 1 more minute, or until the shrimp is firm and completely opaque. Turn off the heat and remove the shrimp to the paper-towel-lined plate to drain.

Scoop the garlic out of the pan with a spoon and discard. Add the limoncello, wine, chives, and lemon juice to the pan. Turn the heat to medium-low, bring the mixture to a simmer, and give it a stir; cook until it reduces to a just a few spoonfuls of sweet, thickened sauce, 2 to 3 minutes. Remove from the heat.

Divide the shrimp between two plates. Spoon the sauce over it, and sprinkle with the parsley. Sprinkle the lemon zest over all.

12	large deveined shrimp, with the tail (8 to 10 ounces)
2 TABLESPOONS	extra-virgin olive oil
2 CLOVES	garlic, roughly chopped into several big chunks
1 TABLESPOON	chopped onion (optional)
¼ CUP	limoncello
¼ CUP	dry white wine, such as Pinot Grigio
1 TABLESPOON	chopped fresh chives
1 TEASPOON	chopped fresh Italian parsley
	Juice and finely grated zest of ½ lemon

JACK'S TURKEY MEATBALLS

IN TOMATO SAUCE

SERVES 4 TO 6

	1 recipe Uncle Hector's Tomato Sauce (page 80)
	MEATBALLS
1⅓ POUNDS	ground (93% lean) turkey
½	Vidalia onion, or 1 small onion, grated to a pulp on the fine holes of a grater
I CUP	finely grated Parmesan cheese
2 TABLESPOONS	finely grated pecorino cheese
2 TABLESPOONS	chopped fresh Italian parsley
5	largish basil leaves, chopped
¾ CUP	fresh bread crumbs (3 slices white bread, crusts removed, ground in food processor), or dried
2 TABLESPOONS	ketchup
FEW DROPS	Worcestershire sauce
½ TEASPOON	garlic powder
I TEASPOON	salt
I	large egg, beaten with a fork
¼ TO ½ CUP	extra-virgin olive oil

Spaghetti and meatballs is *the* archetypal Italian meal and probably the dish that's most associated with the Chef Boyardee brand. I often get requests to teach it. It's not typical of our cuisine because beef wasn't traditionally raised in Piacenza, but this recipe somehow found its way into my Nonna Anna's hands, and she taught my mother.

I always try to have meatballs on hand. You know the way some people keep cold cuts in the "meats" drawer of the fridge? That's how I keep turkey meatballs. Jack loves them and will eat them in almost any form—as is; with pasta; or his own personal favorite, layered on top of a fried egg, on toasted English muffin. In fact, turkey meatballs figured prominently in the early days of our relationship. He was the classic bachelor when I met him: he worked like a fiend, often late, and didn't have the time or inclination to cook for himself. But I noticed that he always had turkey meatballs, purchased from a deli down the street, in his fridge. "What's with the meatballs?" I asked one day. Well, it turns out that they were perfect late-night, no-time-even-to-go-out-to-eat food. So I said, "I'm going to make my turkey meatballs for you." And the rest, as they say, is history.

The meatballs don't need to be served with pasta—Italians traditionally eat them as is, with the sauce (and there are always English muffins), but if you would like to, boil some up (spaghetti is the obvious choice, but you could use anything), and double the tomato sauce.

IN A LARGE SAUCEPAN (it will need to hold both sauce and meatballs), make the tomato sauce according to the recipe on page 80, but cook it only 30 to 35 minutes. Set aside.

Meanwhile, make the meatballs. Line a baking sheet with aluminum foil. Line another baking sheet or large plate with paper towels. Put the ground turkey in a large mixing bowl and gently pull it apart with a fork. Add the grated onion, Parmesan, pecorino, chopped herbs, bread crumbs, ketchup, Worcestershire sauce, and garlic powder, and work gently with the fork to mix the ingredients thoroughly. Gently mix in the salt, and then the beaten egg. Using your hands, roll the mixture into balls a little smaller than a golf ball, and place them on the foil-lined baking sheet.

For a hot meal that's cool to fix...

No need to steam up the kitchen—or yourself—to serve your family the good hot meal nutrition experts say they need, even on a midsummer day.

Simply reach for a can of Chef Boy-Ar-Dee Spaghetti and Meat Balls. Heat. It's ready in minutes. And it has that rare, real-Italian flavor that's so hard to get.

Notice the strands as you dish it up. Perfectly tender, but not mushy or soft. And sniff that wonderful savory sauce—rich with bright tomato and special Italian spices. Then, to top it off, tender beef meat balls—brown outside, juicy inside.

The kids will call it a *cool* dish. You'll call it delicious. Only 13¢ a serving, in 2-serving and 5-serving cans.

It's Chef's special way with sauces that makes this—and *all* Chef meals—so specially good. You can get the sauces separately, too. Try them. Let Chef do the cooking!

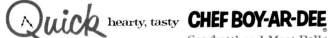 **Quick** hearty, tasty **CHEF BOY-AR-DEE**
Spaghetti and Meat Balls

Heat ¼ cup of the olive oil over medium heat in a large nonstick skillet. Add as many meatballs as will fit comfortably in the pan and cook, turning, until nicely browned, about 6 minutes. Drain them on the paper-towel-lined plate. Add more meatballs to the skillet, and a little oil if the pan is dry, and cook them in the same way. Continue until all the meatballs are cooked and draining.

Gently add the meatballs to the saucepan with the sauce. Bring the sauce to a gentle simmer and cook 20 minutes longer.

THE TWIST

My mom adapted this recipe from her mother-in-law's meatballs. She substituted ground turkey for ground chuck because my brother and I didn't like beef (I still don't care much for red meat). And I'm sure the ketchup was her inspiration, used in place of the more usual tomato paste. That ketchup may account for why my brother and I loved these so much and why my little niece and nephew are happy to help my mom make them when they come over for dinner.

Grating the onion is easier than chopping, and it guarantees no discernible chunks of onion in the meatballs.

CHRISTMAS ROAST CAPON

SERVES 6 TO 8

Christmas was a big deal in my house growing up, with all of us in the neighborhood getting together to celebrate. We were usually about twenty-five people for Christmas dinner—two long tables of contented eaters. Everyone would show up at about seven o'clock to eat, and after dinner, we'd all go to Midnight Mass together. I particularly looked forward to hanging out with my best friend, Paola, who was originally from Milan (it's her father who likes to fish in Sardinia). Sometimes we made Christmas dinner at our house, sometimes at her house, and then we'd all go over to somebody else's house for New Year's Eve.

Christmas was all about food, of course. For several weeks beforehand, my mom and I would have been rolling tons of pasta, enough to assemble a great number of individual, homemade lasagne in little tins. We wrapped the them in beautiful holiday paper, attached cooking instructions, and gave them out to friends as gifts.

Closer to the actual event, the moms in the neighborhood would spend days and days shopping, and cooking, and talking, and house decorating. Paola and I would help with the eating and table setting. My mom made sure that the house was head-to-toe decorated: we put up the Christmas tree in the living room. There were garlands of greenery winding up the main staircase and potted poinsettias in every corner. Candles—wrapped in wide, velvet ribbons that were color coordinated with the year's table centerpiece—were placed on every surface.

The meal began with antipasto and lasagne, and continued with capon and vegetables, and then salad. (And dessert, of course.) Capon was more expensive than chicken, and my grandparents reserved it for special occasions, like Christmas. We've continued the tradition. A capon is a castrated rooster (a less-than-appetizing concept, but the process makes the meat particularly tasty). It's a large bird—7 to 10 pounds—and in Italy, we call it "the king of poultry" because its flavor is so special. We stuff it with fresh rosemary and baste it in buttery drippings. My mom's moist mushroom-onion-sausage stuffing (page 130) bakes separately. I actually prefer capon to turkey (the meat is juicier), and if there are only a few of us at Thanksgiving, I lobby for it. But Jack will never let me get away with it because that's *his* family's tradition.

I don't like a lot of gravy, and the capon is delicious without it, but for the gravy lovers at our table, I've included it in the recipe.

I (7½-POUND)	*capon, preferably organic*
	Salt and freshly ground pepper
½	*onion*
4½	*large carrots*
½	*lemon*
I CLOVE	*garlic, smashed with the heel of your hand or a large knife, and peeled*
4 (4- TO 5-INCH) SPRIGS	*fresh rosemary*
1½ TABLESPOONS	*extra-virgin olive oil, plus extra for the pan*
	Canned, low-sodium chicken broth, if needed in addition to pan drippings
I TABLESPOON	*all-purpose flour*
KITCHEN STUFF	
	Bulb baster
	Degreasing cup

SHOPPING WITH ANNA
You'll probably need to order capon from your butcher, so leave plenty of time for it to arrive. And ask for organic. . . . It's more expensive, but it's worth it for the flavor. If you can't find a local provider, you can order it online from Dartagnan.com.

I used to worry about what would happen when I got married and had to split Christmas between the two families. . . . Well, we all survived. But I make sure that there's a capon roasting, sometime, somewhere, during the holidays.

REMOVE THE INNARDS from the capon. You can either throw them away or do as my mother does, which is to rinse and dry the neck, heart, and gizzard, place them in a resealable freezer bag, and freeze them for chicken broth (page 40). Pull out and discard the clumps of fat around the opening of the cavity. Rinse the capon, inside and out, under cold water until the water running out of the bird is no longer pink. Pat the capon dry with paper towels very well, inside and out, and place it, breast side up, on a sheet of aluminum foil.

Fold the wing tips behind the wings so that they don't burn. Rub the inside of the capon with ¾ teaspoon salt and ⅛ teaspoon pepper. Stuff the capon with the onion half, the ½ carrot, the lemon half, the garlic, and 1 of the rosemary sprigs. To tie the legs of the capon together, cut a piece of string about 12 inches long. Wrap one end around one "ankle," leaving 2 to 3 inches string free at that end, and wrap the other end around the other "ankle" the same way. Pull the loose ends of the string together to cross the "ankles," then tie a knot. Sprinkle the capon all over with about 1¼ teaspoons salt and ⅛ teaspoon pepper. Rub the bird well all over, back and front, with the oil.

Rub the bottom and sides of a small roasting pan with oil. Line up the 4 remaining carrots on the bottom of the pan and set the capon, breast side up, on top. Break the remaining 3 sprigs of rosemary into 1-inch pieces and scatter them over the capon, tucking a couple between the legs and body, and let the capon stand 1 hour at room temperature to absorb all those great tastes.

Preheat the oven to 400°F and arrange a rack in the bottom third. Roast the capon until an instant-read thermometer inserted into the thickest part of the thigh registers 175°F and the juices run clear when you insert a small knife into the thigh, about 2½ hours. When the juices start to accumulate in the pan (1 to 1½ hours into the cooking), baste with a bulb baster, and continue basting every 30 minutes until the capon is cooked. After 1½ hours cooking, when the breast is nice and golden brown, cover it with a sheet of aluminum foil to keep the skin from browning too much.

When you remove the cooked capon from the oven, cover it with a sheet of heavy-duty aluminum foil and let it rest 20 to 30 minutes.

To make the sauce, use the bulb baster to remove all the juices from the pan. Defat the liquid in a degreasing cup, or bring it to a simmer in a small sauce-pan and skim off the fat with a spoon. Measure out 2¼ cups juices; if you don't have enough, add some chicken broth. Pour ¼ cup of the juices into a small saucepan and place it over low heat. Add the flour and whisk until smooth. Bring the sauce to a simmer over medium-high heat, whisking; it will thicken. Add the remaining 2 cups juices. Bring to a simmer and cook until thickened, 3 to 5 minutes. Taste for seasoning; set aside.

To serve the capon, cut off the legs with poultry shears. Cut between the thighs and drumsticks. Slice the breast meat off the carcass with a large, sharp knife. Shingle the breast slices down the center of a pretty platter and put the leg quarters alongside. Rewarm the sauce and drizzle a little over the meat. Pour the rest into a sauceboat and serve it alongside the capon.

APPLE CIDER–ROSEMARY
ROAST CHICKEN

SERVES 2 TO 4

1 (3¼- TO 3½-POUND)	chicken, preferably organic
1 CUP	apple cider vinegar
	Salt and freshly ground pepper
1 CLOVE	garlic, unpeeled, smashed with the side of a large knife
½	lemon
2 SPRIGS	fresh rosemary
2 TABLESPOONS	extra-virgin olive oil
4	medium carrots
4	inner stalks celery
1	onion, peeled and quartered
	KITCHEN STUFF
	Medium-sized roasting pan
	Kitchen shears

Last time we cooked this together, I asked my mother where this recipe came from. We were in my kitchen, and she was tossing a pinch of salt over her left shoulder (into the sink—tradition is one thing, messiness another). The salt-over-the-shoulder toss is an old Italian custom—"Otherwise they say it's bad luck," she says cheerfully. (By this I gather that she's not entirely *convinced* that it's meaningful, but why take the chance?)

Tradition satisfied, I lift the chicken out of its apple cider vinegar bath, and pat it dry with paper towels.

"I'm not really sure where it comes from," she said. "It's just . . . I guess it's just the tips and tricks from everyone's best roast chicken recipe, handed down from one generation to the next."

Once the chicken is well dried, I carefully massage olive oil, salt, and pepper into the skin. This is one of those tricks my mother was talking about: the massaging is supposed to help the seasoning enter into the skin and flesh, and make the skin crisp. Does it work? I don't know. Scientifically, I mean. But I like doing it; massaging the flesh is wonderfully tactile, and the chicken always comes out of the oven crisp-skinned and well seasoned. So I do it. But the salt goes onto the chicken, not over my shoulder.

One thing I *do* know: the use of apple cider vinegar is *very* Italian. We consider vinegar to be extremely healthful, even curative; my doctor in Italy actually prescribed it for my skin one year. And it seems to add a special, subtle flavor to the meat. You can forgo the vegetables, but I don't because they turn the chicken into a one-pot dinner and keep it from swimming in the drippings while it roasts.

REMOVE THE INNARDS, if any; throw them away or save them for stock (see page 40). Place the chicken in a bowl large enough to hold it comfortably, with room to spare. Add the vinegar and enough cold water to cover the chicken completely. Let the chicken soak for about 30 minutes. Remove the chicken from the bowl, rinse it under cold running water, and pat it completely dry, inside and out, with paper towels.

Arrange the oven rack in the bottom third of the oven and preheat the oven to 400°F.

In a roasting pan or baking dish just large enough to hold it, set the chicken, neck end down, so that you are holding its legs in the air. Sprinkle the cavity with about ¾ teaspoon salt and ¼ teaspoon pepper. Add the garlic, the lemon half, and a 4-inch sprig of rosemary. Tie the legs of the chicken together: Cut a piece of string about 12 inches long. Wrap one end around one "ankle," leaving 2 to 3 inches of the string free, and the other end around the other "ankle." Pull the ends of the string to pull together the "ankles," then tie the ends together and knot. Lay the bird in the pan on its breast. Working all over the back (including the backs of the legs and the wings), rub the chicken with about 1½ teaspoons salt until the salt begins to dissolve into the skin. This will take a few minutes; it's fun. Then drizzle on 1 tablespoon of the oil, and rub that all over. Be sure not to miss any nooks and crannies. Rub with about ¼ teaspoon pepper. Now turn the bird breast side up, and repeat the entire operation with another 1½ teaspoons salt, the remaining 1 tablespoon olive oil, and ¼ teaspoon pepper.

Peel the carrots and the bumpy side of the celery ribs with a vegetable peeler. Remove the chicken from the pan and line up carrots and celery sticks (I alternate, but it doesn't matter) in the bottom of the pan. Set an onion quarter in each corner and set the chicken, breast side up, on top of the vegetables. Now tear up a 6-inch sprig of rosemary into 1-inch pieces and scatter them over the top of the chicken.

Put the pan in the oven and roast until the skin of the chicken is nicely browned and the juices run clear when you insert a small knife into the thigh, 1 hour to 1 hour 20 minutes. Remove the pan from the oven, cover the chicken with aluminum foil, and let it rest 15 to 20 minutes.

Uncover the chicken and cut it into 8 pieces with kitchen scissors. Cut the vegetables into pieces with a knife. Arrange the chicken in the center of a casserole or serving bowl and spoon the vegetables around it.

CHICKEN CACCIATORE

SERVES 4

This traditional chicken stew was a favorite of both my grandfather and Uncle Hector, who used to rave about how moist the chicken was. They served it with polenta to soak up the tomato sauce, which picks up the flavor of the chicken, as well as the fresh rosemary and sage. If you don't have (or like) polenta, the stew is also traditionally served with rice cooked in chicken broth, and we also like it with mashed potatoes.

This is definitely more of a winter dish. And it's a great thing to make ahead: the chicken tastes even better the next day, when it's had a chance to absorb some of the sauce.

DUMP THE TOMATOES into a bowl and break them into small pieces with your fingers; set them aside.

Place the chicken pieces in a large bowl and add cold water to cover. Add the vinegar and set aside to soak for 20 minutes.

Place the flour on a large plate or on a sheet of aluminum foil. Arrange another sheet of aluminum foil next to it. Remove the chicken from the cider mixture and dry it very well with paper towels. Working in batches, dredge the chicken in the flour, pat off the excess, and place it in a single layer on the foil. Sprinkle on both sides with the salt and pepper.

In a large, deep (preferably nonstick) skillet with a lid, heat ¼ cup of the olive oil over medium-high heat. Working in batches, add as many chicken pieces as will fit in a single layer. Set your timer for 4 minutes and cook until the pieces are nicely browned. Turn the chicken, set the timer for 4 more minutes, and brown the other sides. Remove the cooked chicken to a plate or baking dish and continue to brown the remaining chicken pieces. (If the pan gets dry, add another tablespoon oil. And make sure that any browned bits on the bottom of the pan don't burn; if they get dark, turn the heat down.) Set the chicken aside.

Turn the heat down to medium. Add the chopped onion, carrot, and celery to the skillet and stir well with a wooden spoon to coat the vegetables with the fat remaining in the pan. Set the timer for 5 minutes and cook until the vegetables are tender. Add the chopped rosemary and sage and cook 2 more minutes.

1½ CUPS	*(about 5) canned, drained Italian peeled plum tomatoes*
1 (4- TO 5- POUND)	*chicken, skinned and cut into small (about 3-inch) pieces, with bone, thighs, and wings left whole (ask your butcher to do this for you or use kitchen scissors)*
½ CUP	*apple cider vinegar*
½ CUP	*all-purpose flour*
2 TEASPOONS	*salt*
½ TEASPOON	*freshly ground pepper*
4 TO 5 TABLESPOONS	*extra-virgin olive oil*
1	*small onion, chopped*
1	*carrot, finely chopped*
1 STALK	*celery, pulled from the interior of the bunch (they're more tender), finely chopped*
NEEDLES FROM 2 SMALL SPRIGS	*fresh rosemary, finely chopped (about 1½ teaspoons)*
2	*large fresh sage leaves, finely chopped (about 1 teaspoon)*
½ CUP	*chicken broth (canned low-sodium is fine!)*

Return all the chicken to the pan and stir well to coat with the vegetable mixture. Cook 3 minutes. Add the chopped tomatoes and stir well. Add the chicken broth, bring to a boil, reduce the heat, cover the pan, and set the timer for 1 hour. Let the stew simmer very gently until the timer rings—it will be tender and super moist.

THE TWIST

This stew would traditionally been made with chicken and its skin. We pull off the skin to reduce the fat, and the flavor is still very wonderful, but if you aren't concerned about fat, you can leave the skin on.

CHICKEN CUTLETS

WITH HAM, CHEESE, TOMATOES, AND CAPERS

SERVES 4

In Piacenza, this is a common, everyday way to prepare chicken using ingredients we cook with a lot. I teach it because it's an easy dish for beginners to master and my students think it's something special (I don't tell them otherwise). I often make it for my yearly Christmas party because it's easy to do ahead. You can assemble it several hours in advance, put it aside, and still have something hot coming out of the oven when guests arrive.

LINE A BAKING SHEET with aluminum foil. If you have a meat pounder, this is the time to get it out; otherwise, use an empty wine bottle. Set one of the chicken breasts on a sheet of plastic wrap and cover it with another sheet of plastic wrap. Pound with your meat pounder or the side of the wine bottle until the chicken gets as thin and as flat as possible. It will shred a bit as it thins and it may even develop some holes . . . that's okay. Do the same with the rest of the chicken. Now cut the breasts into rectangles 2 or 3 inches wide and about 4 inches long. The pieces will be irregularly shaped, and that's just fine.

Place the flour on a large plate. Set a 9-by-13-inch baking dish next to the stove.

In a large skillet, heat the butter with the olive oil over medium heat until the butter melts. Turn several of the chicken pieces in the flour to coat, pat off the excess, and place in the pan. Add enough chicken to fit without crowding. Cook the chicken until it is golden brown, 2 to 3 minutes each side. Use a spatula to remove the chicken to the baking dish. Flour and cook the rest of the chicken, making sure not to do too many at a time, and place in the baking dish.

Add the wine to pan and boil until the sauce is reduced by about one half and slightly thickened, 5 to 7 minutes.

Preheat the oven to 350°F and center a rack in the oven.

Meanwhile, tear the ham into pieces about the size of the chicken cutlets and cover each piece of chicken with a piece of ham. Cut the cheese into pieces of equal size and layer them on top of the ham. Top each with a slice of tomato and 3 or 4 capers. Spoon the sauce over the chicken to moisten it. Bake the chicken until the cheese melts, about 15 minutes.

1¼ POUNDS	boneless, skinless chicken breast
⅓ CUP	all-purpose flour
3 TABLESPOONS	unsalted butter
3 TABLESPOONS	extra-virgin olive oil
½ CUP	dry white wine such as Pinot Grigio
4	very thin pieces good-quality boiled ham
¼ POUND	Fontina cheese, thinly sliced, or 4 to 6 slices American cheese
3	plum tomatoes cut into 10 (⅓-inch-thick) round slices
2 TABLESPOONS	drained nonpareil capers (the tiny ones)

CHICKEN GABRIELLA

SERVES 4

My dad brought the family to the States when I was five. Before we moved, he came over to New York on his own to look for a house. One night, as he tells the story, he was playing poker with some guys in one of the players' apartments in Manhattan. They're all sitting around the table, and one fellow says, "What are you doing here?"

"I've got a wife and children in Italy and I'm looking for a place to live."

"I've got a nice piece of property in New Jersey," the fellow says. "I've been promoted, and I have to move and sell the property."

"Well, I'll go over and take a look at it," says my dad.

It was a nice piece of land. He bought it and built a house on it, and I grew up there. The name of the fellow who sold it to him was Joe Namath.

We were lucky in that many of our friends from Italy also moved into our neighborhood in New Jersey. We all lived within about five miles of one another. My mom's friend Gabriella lived across the street. She's a fabulous cook. I tasted this lemony rosemary-and-sage chicken stew at her house one night and promptly asked her to show me how to make it. It's now a staple in my own kitchen. Serve it with rice to soak up the sauce, or with roasted potatoes.

PUT THE CHICKEN PIECES in a 12-inch skillet (preferably nonstick) with a lid, along with the chopped onions, rosemary, and sage. Stir well to coat the chicken with the onion and herbs. Add enough olive oil to coat all of the chicken pieces, but not so much that it pools in the skillet. Sprinkle with ¾ teaspoon salt and ¼ teaspoon pepper.

Set the skillet over medium heat. Cook until the onions are very soft and the chicken and onions have turned golden brown, about 20 minutes. If the onion begins to brown too fast, turn down the heat.

Add the wine and bring to a boil. Reduce the heat, cover the pan, and simmer gently until the chicken is tender, about 20 minutes. Squeeze the lemon over, taste for salt and pepper, and serve.

1 (3½- TO 4-POUND)	chicken, skinned and cut into small (about 3-inch) pieces, with bone, thighs, and wings left whole (ask your butcher to do this for you or use kitchen shears)
2	onions, chopped
NEEDLES FROM 4 SPRIGS	fresh rosemary (about ¼ cup), finely chopped
5	fresh sage leaves, finely chopped
ABOUT ¼ CUP	extra-virgin olive oil
	Salt and freshly ground pepper
1 CUP	dry white wine, such as Pinot Grigio
1	lemon

BREAD STUFFING

SERVES 6 TO 8

1 LARGE LOAF (1 POUND)	*sliced white bread*
¾ POUND	*cremini (also called baby portobello) mushrooms*
8 TABLESPOONS	*extra-virgin olive oil*
1 POUND	*luganica sausage, removed from casing*
2 CUPS	*chopped onion (from about 2 onions)*
3 CUPS	*coarsely chopped celery (about 4 inner stalks, with leaves)*
	Salt and freshly ground pepper
1 CLOVE	*garlic, chopped*
3 TABLESPOONS	*chopped fresh Italian parsley*
2	*small carrots, grated (optional)*
1½ CUPS	*canned low-sodium chicken broth*
1 CUP	*finely grated Parmesan cheese*
1½ TABLESPOONS	*unsalted butter, plus extra for the baking dish*
¼ CUP	*drippings from a roasting bird (optional)*

The family traditionally serves this mushroom-sausage stuffing at Christmas and Thanksgiving. But it will also turn an everyday roast chicken dinner into a special affair. The recipe doubles or triples easily, depending on how many mouths you're feeding. (Be forewarned: We generally double it, and there's still never enough.) A flat wooden spoon is particularly good for breaking up the sausage.

The stuffing can be assembled up to two days in advance and refrigerated until you're ready to cook. Bring it to room temperature before baking. Then, when the capon is cooked, remove the bird from the oven, reduce the oven heat, and bake the stuffing.

PREHEAT THE OVEN to 250°F. Working with a stack of three slices at a time, cut the crusts off the bread slices with a serrated knife and cut the slices into nine cubes. Place the cubes on a baking sheet and bake until they are crisp and dry, but not browned, 25 to 30 minutes. Dump the bread cubes into a large bowl.

Meanwhile, wipe the mushrooms clean with a damp paper towel and trim the stems. Slice, and set aside in a bowl.

Heat 1 tablespoon of the oil in a large (12-inch is perfect) skillet over medium heat. Add the sausage meat and cook, breaking it up into small pieces with a wooden spoon, until it's no longer pink and begins to brown on the outside, 7 to 10 minutes. Remove it to the bowl with the toasted bread using a slotted spoon.

Discard the fat from the skillet and adjust the heat to medium-low. Add 3 more tablespoons oil, and when it's hot, add the chopped onion and cook until softened, about 5 minutes. Add the celery. Sprinkle lightly with salt and a pinch of pepper. Cook until the vegetables are very soft, about 10 more minutes. Add them to the bowl with the bread.

Return the skillet to the stove and increase the heat to medium-high. Add ¼ cup oil and heat until it's good and hot. Spread the sliced mushrooms over the bottom of the pan and let them cook, without stirring, until they give up their liquid and the liquid has evaporated, 8 to 10 minutes. (You can nudge them a bit to keep them evenly layered in the skillet, but don't stir, or they won't cook.) Stir in ⅛ teaspoon salt and the chopped garlic and cook 2 more minutes. Add the cooked mushrooms, the parsley, and grated carrot, if using, to the bowl with everything else and give it all a good stir.

Bring the broth to a simmer (you can use the skillet). Gradually add it to the bowl, mixing gently until the bread is moistened but not wet and is just beginning to fall apart. Let cool. Stir in the cheese. Taste to see if the stuffing needs salt or pepper.

Preheat the oven to 350°F. Butter an oven-to-table casserole, preferably something large and shallow so there's lots of surface area for browning (a 9-by-13-inch baking dish works fine). Spoon the stuffing into the casserole and smooth the top. Dot with the butter. Bake 15 minutes. Using a bulb baster, drizzle the top of the stuffing with some of the drippings from the capon or turkey you may be roasting (you'll want to use about ¼ cup, all told) and continue baking until the top of the stuffing is golden brown, about 15 more minutes.

NONNA ANNA'S
POLENTA PASTICCIATA

SERVES 6 TO 8

1 RECIPE	*Mushroom Sauce (page 84)*
1 RECIPE	*Polenta (page 63)*
½ CUP	*finely grated Parmesan cheese*
1¼ CUPS	*coarsely shredded Fontina, or fresh or packaged mozzarella cheese (about 5 ounces)*
1 TABLESPOON	*unsalted butter, cut into bits, plus additional for the dish*

Like my dad, my Nonna Anna was a wonderful storyteller, and I was generally prepared to listen. Endlessly. This dish of baked polenta, layered like a lasagne with a tomatoey mushroom sauce and two cheeses, was one of the recipes we used to like to cook together. I could usually get her to tell me (again) the stories of how she and her mother ended up in the States, and how she met my grandfather.

She was born in the remote, mountainous region of Perino, southwest of Piacenza. It was a hard place to make a living, and the once-large family gradually left home to find work elsewhere (her dad emigrated to Pennsylvania to work in the coal mines). Eventually, only my grandmother (the youngest child) and her mother were left. With no hope of finding work, her mother decided they would have to leave home, too.

Stuffing her pockets with salami for the voyage, she took the child to the port of Genoa and told the ticket man she wanted to go to America. He, not knowing which America she was talking about, said, "Buenos Aires? Or New York?"

"I want to go where I can find work to feed my child," she said.

So he sold her tickets to New York. They got a place to live downtown on Baxter Street, not too far from where I live now. Her mom found work going around to restaurants to gather and repair tablecloths and napkins. My grandmother's first job was making hats; later on, she worked in a factory rolling cigars.

My grandparents met in New York, at a community dance. Nonna Anna was a great dancer, and she and my grandfather used to love going out dancing. By the time I knew her, she had the means to outfit herself luxuriously—I remember racks of incredibly fancy dresses, mink stoles, and outrageous jewelry.

But she never forgot Perino and those sausages, which her mother rationed out over the course of the journey to New York. Her stories always ended with "See, Anna? Food is so important. You must be grateful for food and tradition."

Pasticciata means "messy mixture" in Italian, and this dish can be mixed up in lots of different ways. It's nice to replace the Fontina with Gorgonzola cheese, or use a regular tomato sauce (page 80) in place of the mushroom sauce. Or layer it with Bolognese (page 92) and besciamella sauces (page 95), like you're making a true lasagne.

SEAFOOD, POULTRY, AND MEATS

Most Americans have never eaten this, so it's appealingly exotic. Recently, I sent Jack off with a piece for his sister Kelli's lunch. Kelli is very Americana, which makes her the perfect recipe *taster*. She'd never eaten polenta at all. I got a very funny e-mail from her after lunch: "I have no idea what this is, but it's delicious." I think you'll find that your guests will have a similar reaction. It's cheesy and starchy and tomatoey. . . . What's not to like?

MAKE THE MUSHROOM SAUCE and set it aside.

While the sauce cooks, make the polenta.

While the polenta is still warm, preheat the oven to 350°F. Center a rack in the oven. Butter the bottom and sides of a 9-by-13-inch baking dish.

Coat the bottom of the dish with enough mushroom sauce to cover. Sprinkle it with about 2 tablespoons of the Parmesan and ¼ cup of the Fontina. Spoon about half of the warm polenta into the dish and smooth it into an even layer. Spoon half of the remaining sauce over the polenta in a smooth layer. Sprinkle with 3 more tablespoons Parmesan cheese and about ⅓ cup of the Fontina. Pour the rest of the polenta on top and smooth it with the spoon to level it. Pour on the rest of the sauce, spreading it so that the polenta is entirely covered. Sprinkle with 3 more tablespoons Parmesan and the remaining ⅔ cup Fontina. Dot all over the top with bits of butter.

Bake the pasticciata until a little golden-brown crust forms on top, about 30 minutes. Remove it from the oven and let stand for 5 minutes to firm up before serving.

POLENTA PASTICCIATA WITH SAUSAGE

Sometimes I substitute sausage for the mushroom sauce: Cook 1 pound fresh Italian link sausage in a skillet over medium heat. Turn it every now and then until it's nicely browned and the juices run clear when you poke the sausages with the point of a small knife, about 10 minutes. Slice it and layer it in place of the sauce.

BOLLITO MISTO

SERVES 4 TO 6

Bollito misto (rather less glamorous-sounding in English . . . it means "mixed boil") is a perfect example of the kind of simple, inexpensive, and uncomplicated food that generations of Boiardis grew up on: beef, poultry, and vegetables simmered in water. The meats are served with a peppy sauce of chopped fresh parsley, onion, and olive oil. My dad is such a great fan of this sauce that he regularly volunteers to chop the onions. *His* father, Mario, loved it too; Mario perked up his version of the sauce with chopped anchovies and capers.

The broth is traditionally served separately with a homemade pasta called anolini (page 107), but it also makes a good base for soup, risotti, and other pastas.

I associate this recipe with Nonna Anna's stories of the war years, when the family shut down civilian operation at the Chef Boyardee plant and converted it to work for the government, making rations for Allied troops. The company made every conceivable type of canned food (they beat out Campbell's Soup to win a contract for canned breakfasts!). The plant was operating around the clock, and my grandfather and Uncle Hector spent most of their time there, only coming home to eat and grab some rest before dashing back to the factory. Nonna Anna made a point of having bollito misto in the refrigerator. With the broth and bits of boiled meat and vegetables, she could always pull together something hot and nourishing—soup, pasta, or risotto—whatever time of day or night the men showed up.

Somewhere in the telling of the story, my grandmother would always pause to encourage me to keep homemade chicken broth in my refrigerator when I had my own family. I do. (Not always. But mostly.)

I think the war experience finally slowed the brothers down. At the war's end, facing the daunting prospect of retooling this now-substantial company—five thousand strong, at that point—for a civilian market, the family merged with American Home Foods in 1945. Hector stayed on as a consultant until 1978.

But the brothers maintained a great fondness for this dish. After the war, they made yearly visits to Piacenza by cruise liner, docking at Genoa and driving the rest of the way in their enormous Lincoln Continental. Their first stop off the ship was at a local restaurant in the town of Tortona, about halfway between Genoa and Piacenza, where they'd sit down to a meal of bollito. I make it in the winter, when the steaming broth, which takes on

	BOLLITO
	½ fowl (about 3 pounds), or 1 chicken
2 POUNDS	beef chuck roast
1	onion, peeled and trimmed, but left whole
1	carrot, peeled and trimmed, but left whole
1 STALK	celery, trimmed and left whole
15 CUPS	cold water
1 TABLESPOON	salt
	SALSA VERDE (PARSLEY SAUCE)
2 FIRMLY PACKED CUPS	fresh Italian parsley leaves
1	medium red onion, finely chopped (½ cup)
¼ CUP	extra-virgin olive oil
½ TEASPOON	salt
¼ TEASPOON	freshly ground pepper
1 TABLESPOON	drained nonpareil capers (the tiny ones; optional)

SEAFOOD, POULTRY, AND MEATS

Award ceremony for the presentation of the "E" flag by the United States government. Chef Boyardee was the second food company to receive this award.

SEAFOOD, POULTRY, AND MEATS

such wonderful flavors from the meats and vegetables, makes the house smell cozy.

Put the fowl, chuck, onion, carrot, and celery into a large soup pot. Add water to cover (the traditional proportion is 3 cups water to 1 pound meat, but you can use less water for a stronger-tasting stock, if you like—just make sure the water covers the meat). Bring to a boil over medium-high heat. Set a bowl next to the stove. As the water heats, the fat and a bunch of gray scum will gradually float to the top. Skim off the scum with a skimmer or a large spoon, putting it into the bowl. You'll be skimming for a while—15 or 20 minutes, intermittently.

Once the water looks pretty clear, add the salt, and reduce the heat so that the water simmers. Cover and cook until the beef is soft enough to cut with a fork, about 2½ hours.

FOR THE SALSA VERDE, put the chopped parsley, red onion, oil, salt, and pepper in a bowl. Add the capers, if using, and stir well to mix. Cover and set aside at room temperature. (This should sit to allow the flavors to blend for at least 30 minutes, or up to several hours.)

To serve the bollito, carefully remove the meat to a platter with a skimmer or two forks. Add the vegetables. Set a fine strainer over a large bowl or pot. Line the strainer with paper towels, and strain the broth. Cut the meats and vegetables into serving pieces and spoon a little of the hot broth over them. Serve the meats with the parsley sauce.

Pour the broth into containers and refrigerate or freeze it to serve with ano-lini (page 107). Or save it to serve to *your* family and friends, when they arrive home late from the factory.

> ### THE TWIST
> *Bollito misto is traditionally served with salsa verde, but it's quite delicious with store-bought mayonnaise, Dijon mustard, or even cocktail sauce. The meat absolutely does* need *some sauce or other, though; it will taste quite dry without it.*

GRILLED VEAL CHOPS

WITH SAGE

SERVES 4

4	veal chops, preferably on the bone, about 1 inch thick (1½ to 2 pounds total)
1½ TABLESPOONS	extra-virgin olive oil
	Salt and freshly ground pepper
4	large leaves fresh sage, roughly chopped
	Olive oil spray, for grilling
KITCHEN STUFF	
	Stovetop grill pan

It's amazing what a little salt, pepper, and olive oil will do to bring out the flavor in meat. Sage works nicely to spruce up veal chops. You'll need to season these chops at least an hour before you plan to serve them (2 to 3 hours is even better) to give the flavors a little time to get into the meat. You can also season and refrigerate the chops overnight to save time the next day.

I do these on a nonstick stovetop grill pan but if you've got an outdoor grill, that's a good way to go, too.

Serve the chops with baked fennel (page 154), spinach (page 162), or roasted potatoes (page 157). Add a nice, big green salad, and you have a beautiful dinner.

PUT THE CHOPS on a platter. Drizzle half of the oil over the meaty part of the chops and massage it well into the meat. Sprinkle with ½ teaspoon salt and ¼ teaspoon pepper and rub those into the meat. Turn the chops. Drizzle with the remaining olive oil and massage well; sprinkle with ½ teaspoon salt and ¼ teaspoon pepper and rub again. Sprinkle sage on both sides. Cover the chops with plastic and let stand at least 1 hour at room temperature, or refrigerate overnight.

Spray a stovetop grill pan with the cooking spray and heat over medium-high heat. When the pan is hot, add as many chops as will fit easily in a single layer and grill until well marked, about 3 minutes. Turn the chops and grill until the other side is well marked and the veal is barely pink when you cut into it, about 3 more minutes. Remove the meat to a platter. If all the chops didn't fit the first time, continue to grill the rest of the chops the same way.

WELL-PATTED MEAT LOAF

SERVES 4 TO 6

1½ POUNDS	*meat-loaf mix (equal parts ground beef, pork, and veal)*
2	*large eggs*
1	*onion, finely chopped*
3 TABLESPOONS	*chopped fresh Italian parsley*
3½ TABLESPOONS	*ketchup*
1½ TABLESPOONS	*Worcestershire sauce*
2 TEASPOONS	*salt*
¼ TEASPOON	*freshly ground pepper*
1½ CUPS	*plain dried bread crumbs*
1½ TABLESPOONS	*finely grated Parmesan cheese*
1½ TABLESPOONS	*finely grated pecorino cheese*
	Olive oil for the pan

This was my Nonna Anna's recipe for a crusty-on-the-outside, moist-on-the-inside Italian version of meat loaf.

The first time I taught it in one of my classes, I had to giggle. I was showing my students how to form the loaf: I'd shaped it into a rectangle and evened the top. Then, as my grandmother always did, I began to pat. All over the top of the loaf.

"And then you pat the loaf to get the air bubbles out," I was saying.

Pat, pat, pat, pat, pat.

"Air bubbles . . . ?" One of my students stopped me, peering closely to see the bubbles. "In a meat loaf?"

Well, she had a point. I don't know if there are actually any bubbles. But it's a great meat loaf, and I always go with what works.

In the days before anyone had ever heard the term "heart-healthy," Nonna Anna used to toss chunks of carrot and onion in olive oil, salt, and pepper, and scatter the vegetables around the meat loaf in the baking dish. As the meat loaf cooked, she basted the vegetables with the fat and juices that collected in the pan. But I think it's even better with mashed potatoes.

IN A LARGE BOWL, gently combine the three meats with a fork. Break the eggs into another bowl. Add the chopped onion, parsley, 3 tablespoons of the ketchup, the Worcestershire, salt, and pepper and beat with the fork to blend. Add to the bowl with the meat. Add the bread crumbs and grated cheeses and gently work the ingredients together with the fork until blended.

Preheat the oven to 375°F. Rub the bottom of a shallow baking dish or foil lasagne pan with oil. Dump the meat mixture onto the baking dish and shape it with clean hands into a rectangle about 2 inches high, 5 to 6 inches wide, and 10 to 11 inches long. Level the top (for even cooking), and pat it several times "to get the air bubbles out." Use the remaining ½ tablespoon ketchup to coat the top of the loaf, then bake until it is completely cooked through, about 45 minutes. Check the meat loaf after 30 minutes; if it's already developed a crust, cover it with foil for the rest of the cooking time.

Remove the meat loaf from the oven, cover it with foil, and let it stand 10 minutes before cutting it into slices for serving.

BRASATO

SERVES 4 TO 6

Brasato is a chunk of meat cooked gently in a covered pot with vegetables, white wine, and a little broth. This is a good method for cooking an inexpensive cut, such as eye of round, which is very delicious but too tough to throw on the grill. And since most Italian families of my parents' generation didn't have ovens, it was also a practical dish because it could be cooked on top of the stove. Even if you *do* have an oven, it's still a nice wintertime meal, served with polenta.

PUT THE FLOUR on a plate and set it next to the stove. Pat the meat dry with paper towels; set aside.

In a deep pot large enough to hold the meat comfortably, melt the butter with the oil over medium heat until the fat sizzles. Dredge the meat in the flour so that it is completely coated, and pat off the excess. Put the meat in the pot and cook until it is nicely browned on all sides, 5 to 6 minutes per side. Remove the meat from the pot and set it on a plate. Add the chopped vegetables to the pot, reduce the heat to medium-low, and cook, stirring to pick up any browned bits on the bottom of the pot, until softened but not browned, 6 to 7 minutes. Return the meat to the pot with any juices that have accumulated on the plate.

Add the wine and simmer until it evaporates completely. In a measuring cup or small bowl, stir the tomato paste with the broth, and add it to the pot. Add the salt, pepper, bay leaf, and rosemary. Bring to a boil, reduce the heat, and simmer very gently, covered, until the meat is so tender that you can cut it with a fork, 3 to 3½ hours. Check about halfway through cooking to make sure the liquid has not evaporated completely. If the pan looks dry, add a little water.

Remove the meat from the pot. Cut it into slices and put them on a platter. Pour the sauce over.

2 TABLESPOONS	*all-purpose flour*
2½ POUNDS	*beef eye of round roast*
2 TABLESPOONS	*unsalted butter*
2 TABLESPOONS	*extra-virgin olive oil*
½	*onion, chopped*
1	*carrot, chopped*
1 STALK	*celery, chopped*
1 CUP	*dry white wine such as Pinot Grigio*
1 TABLESPOON	*tomato paste*
1 CUP	*canned low-sodium chicken broth*
1 TEASPOON	*salt*
½ TEASPOON	*freshly ground pepper*
1	*bay leaf, cut in half*
1 (3-INCH) SPRIG	*fresh rosemary*

VEAL CUTLETS

WITH ARUGULA AND TOMATOES

SERVES 4

It's traditional in northern Italy to prepare veal cutlets by pounding them thin, breading and sautéing for a crisp crust, and serving them with arugula and a drizzle of lemony vinaigrette. It's a good anytime dish, but it works well for parties, too, because it's easy to do in volume. I set out one platter with the cutlets and another with the salad; the vinaigrette is in a gravy boat on the side.

The cutlets (*scaloppine*, in Italian) are sliced very thin from the leg of the veal. If you can't find cutlets in the meat aisle of the supermarket, ask the supermarket butcher to cut them for you. You can, of course, use chicken cutlets instead, but being Italian, we prefer the veal: it's a little more special and certainly more traditional.

You don't *have* to pound the cutlets if they're thin to begin with. But if you have a mallet with the little points (which makes the mallet look like a medieval battle instrument), it's a good idea to give the cutlets a little whack—it'll make them more tender and allow the garlic-milk marinade to penetrate. The marinade tenderizes and adds a subtle, garlic flavor. Yum!

PUT THE EGG, garlic, milk, salt, and pepper in a baking dish or plastic container and whisk with a fork to blend.

If you have a mallet, set a cutting board on your work surface. Put the cutlets on the board and bang them all over, on both sides, with the mallet until the veal is very thin. Put the cutlets into the container with the milk mixture. (If you don't have a mallet, just put the veal into the milk mixture.) Cover and refrigerate at least 1 hour, or overnight.

When you're ready to cook, put the olive oil and the butter into a large skillet with the rosemary. Set it on the stove, but don't turn on the heat. Put the bread crumbs onto a plate or a large square of aluminum foil and set your container full of veal on one side of it; set a large plate on the other side. With a fork, remove one cutlet at a time from the milk mixture and place it on top of the bread crumbs. Spoon some crumbs over the veal. Turn the veal in the crumbs until it is completely coated with a thin layer. Press the crumbs into the veal with clean hands. Place the finished cutlets on the empty plate.

	VEAL CUTLETS	
1	*large egg*	
1	*clove garlic, crushed with the heel of your hand, and peeled*	
¼ CUP	*milk*	
¼ TEASPOON	*salt*	
PINCH	*freshly ground pepper*	
1 POUND	*veal cutlets, cut very thin*	
3 TABLESPOONS	*extra-virgin olive oil, or as needed*	
3 TABLESPOONS	*unsalted butter*	
2 (3-INCH) SPRIGS	*fresh rosemary*	
1 CUP	*plain, dried bread crumbs*	
	VINAIGRETTE	
	Juice of 1 lemon (about 3 tablespoons)	
½ TEASPOON	*salt*	
PINCH	*freshly ground pepper*	
5 TABLESPOONS	*extra-virgin olive oil*	
4	*ripe plum tomatoes*	
3 OUNCES	*arugula*	

Heat the skillet over medium-low heat until the butter is melted. (Higher heat will toughen the veal.) Cover a large plate with a double layer of paper towels and place it next to the stove. Add as many cutlets to the pan as will fit comfortably (probably three) and cook they until nicely browned on one side, 2 to 3 minutes. Turn them and brown the other side. Remove the veal to the paper-towel-lined plate to drain. Keep cooking until all the veal is cooked, adding a tablespoon more oil if the pan gets dry.

To make the vinaigrette, whisk the lemon juice with the salt and pepper in a small bowl with a fork. Then whisk in the oil, a tablespoon at a time, until thickened.

Slice the tomatoes into rounds or wedges and arrange them around the rim of a platter. Make a bed of the arugula on the platter. Shingle the veal on top of the arugula. Drizzle the veal with some of the vinaigrette and serve the rest at the table.

VEAL ROAST

For my parents' generation, a veal roast was something special to look forward to. Too expensive for everyday dining, the roast was reserved for the holidays, or to celebrate the grape harvest in September.

This roast will serve six hungry people—or eight, after a starter of pasta. Serve it with baked cauliflower (page 153) and roasted potatoes (page 157).

THE DAY BEFORE YOU PLAN TO COOK, set the veal in a bowl. Pour the olive oil over and rub it into the meat all over. Sprinkle the top with 1 teaspoon of the salt, and rub that all over the top of the roast. Turn the roast, sprinkle it with the remaining 1 teaspoon salt, and again rub all over. Sprinkle half of the garlic powder and chopped herbs on the roast and rub. Turn the roast and repeat the sprinkling and rubbing process with the remaining garlic powder and herbs. Pour the wine into the bowl and turn the meat in the wine. Cover and refrigerate it overnight, turning it in the wine whenever you think of it (every couple of hours, except when you're sleeping).

Preheat the oven to 375°F and center a rack in the oven. Place the roast in a baking dish or small roasting pan. Pour the marinade around the meat. Cover it loosely with foil and roast, basting once the meat begins to color (after about 1 hour), until the veal registers 180°F on an instant-read thermometer, 2¼ to 2¾ hours, depending on your oven. Check on the veal halfway through roasting. If the marinade dries out and the bottom of the pan begins to brown, add some of the broth.

When the veal is cooked, remove the roast from the oven and set it on a cutting board. Cover it loosely with foil. Pour the drippings into a small saucepan. (Or, if there isn't very much in the way of drippings, pour the broth into the pan and stir with a wooden spoon, scraping the browned bits on the bottom to incorporate them into the liquid; pour that into a small saucepan.)

Remove and discard the twine from the roast. Cut the roast into ½-inch-thick pieces and arrange them on a serving platter. Bring the sauce to a simmer and spoon it over the meat.

3 TO 3¼ POUNDS	veal roast, cut from the shoulder and neck, and tied with butcher's twine
3 TABLESPOONS	extra-virgin olive oil
2 TEASPOONS	salt
½ TEASPOON	garlic powder
I TABLESPOON	finely chopped fresh rosemary
3 LARGE LEAVES	sage, finely chopped
½ CUP	dry white wine
½ TO I CUP	low-sodium canned chicken broth, as needed

SHOPPING WITH ANNA
Most markets don't carry veal roast. You'll need to special-order it from your supermarket or butcher. The best veal is pale in color.

NEW YEAR'S COTECHINO

WITH LENTILS

SERVES 4 TO 6

2 CUPS	*lentils, preferably Italian or French*
I POUND	*cotechino or other sausage*
4½ TABLESPOONS	*extra-virgin olive oil*
I	*medium onion, chopped to the size of the lentils*
	Salt and freshly ground pepper
I	*medium carrot, chopped to the size of the lentils*
I STALK	*celery (from the inside of the bunch— they're more tender), chopped to the size of the lentils*
3 CLOVES	*garlic, smashed with the heel of your hand and peeled, but left whole*
½ TABLESPOON	*tomato paste*
½	*bay leaf*
2½ CUPS	*canned, low-sodium chicken broth, or as needed*

SHOPPING WITH ANNA

The best lentils are the French or Italian varieties sold at specialty stores.

This dish is very typical of the cuisine of Piacenza, which is famous for a thick, locally produced pork sausage called cotechino. For some unfathomable reason, Italians associate lentils with good luck. In the north, every family serves this dish on New Year's Eve, traditionally with mashed potatoes. My grandparents and their families would have eaten cotechino often, not just for New Year's. My dad loves it.

This combination of lentils and sausage is too delicious to miss; if you can't find cotechino, substitute sweet Italian sausage, or any favorite variety, even turkey sausage. (Poach the sausage just like the cotechino, or grill or broil it.) Or forget the sausage and make the lentils on their own the way I do—they're delicious!

We use whole garlic cloves and remove them as soon as the lentils are cooked to give the dish just a hint of garlic flavor.

PUT THE LENTILS in a bowl and add enough cold water to cover. Cover and set aside at room temperature overnight.

The next day, choose a pot large enough to hold the cotechino. Fill it with enough cold water to cover the sausage completely. Bring the water to a boil (without the sausage). Add the sausage. Cover, and simmer 20 minutes, then turn off the heat and let the pot sit, covered, until you're ready to eat.

Meanwhile, heat the oil in an 8-inch casserole or saucepan over medium-low heat. Add the onion, ⅛ teaspoon salt and ⅛ teaspoon pepper. Stir to coat the onion with the oil, and cook until the onion is translucent, about 8 minutes. Add the carrot and celery, stir, and cook until the vegetables are softened, about 5 minutes. Now add the garlic, stir, and cook 2 minutes. Add the tomato paste and stir well to blend it completely with the vegetables.

Place a colander in the sink. Drain the lentils in the colander, then transfer them to the pan with the vegetables. Stir well and cook about 2 minutes. Add the bay leaf and the broth. The broth should just cover the lentils; add more if necessary. Bring the broth to a boil, reduce the heat, cover the pot, and simmer very gently until the lentils are tender and most of the broth has been absorbed, 30 to 40 minutes. Check the lentils during cooking. If they are dry, add a little water; if they're still brothy once they're cooked, boil them for a few minutes, uncovered, to evaporate the liquid. Remove the garlic cloves and the bay leaf.

To serve, spoon the lentils onto a serving platter. Remove the cotechino with a large fork to a cutting board and cut into ½-inch-thick slices. Shingle the cotechino on top of the lentils and serve.

THE TWIST

In Italy, cotechino is sold uncooked, and it takes 2½ to 3 hours to poach. In America, it's sold precooked. It's hardly an everyday food here, but it's not too difficult to find where Italian meats are sold.

VEGETABLES AND SALADS

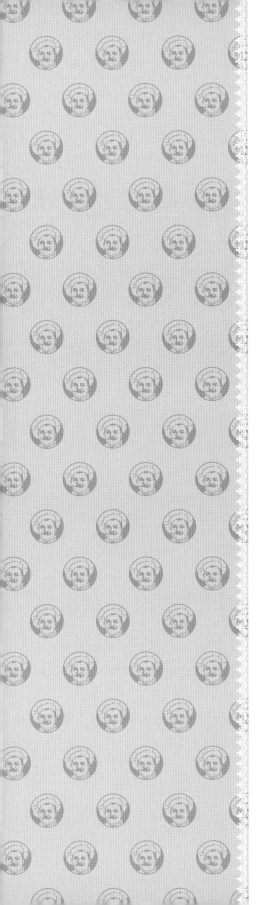

One of the reasons for Piacenza's fantastic culinary reputation is its location (south of Milan, and on the way to Bologna) on the south bank of the Po River. The land there is exceptionally fertile and is excellent for growing all sorts of vegetables, greens, and legumes.

And the vegetables in Italy taste so *good!* We ate tons of cooked vegetables and fresh salads growing up. I wouldn't dream of serving a meal without *some* vegetable (often a salad). My mother wouldn't dream of serving less than two!

All of the salads and some of the vegetable recipes in this chapter also work very nicely as antipasti. The Asparagus alla Parmigiana, for example, can be served chilled, with a lemon vinaigrette. The Peperonata (sautéed pepper strips with sweet onions and capers) is pretty on an antipasto platter, as are the grilled Zucchini Rounds with Oil and Vinegar.

The richer dishes, such as Baked Cauliflower, Buttery Spinach with Parmesan Cheese, Stuffed Zucchini Boats, and Baked Fennel with Parmesan Cheese and Butter, show themselves best when paired with a plain roast—veal, chicken, or capon.

The Plain Roasted Butternut Squash and Buttery Spinach with Parmesan Cheese are particularly nice with branzino, because their colors pop against the white of the fish.

These recipes are the stuff of everyday home cooking, which is to say really, *really*, REALLY doable. But I serve them all when I entertain, and the crowds are enthusiastic. So don't be afraid to show them off, either. They're pretty and colorful, and people love them.

FIRST-IN-LINE GREEN BEANS

SERVES 4

1 POUND	green beans, ends trimmed
	Salt
¼ CUP	extra-virgin olive oil
1½ TABLESPOONS	chopped fresh Italian parsley
1 CLOVE	garlic, chopped fine
2 TABLESPOONS	red wine vinegar

I entertain a lot. It's not unusual for me to be cooking for ninety to a hundred people (we invite seventy-five, and somehow it turns into a lot more). One of Jack's friends, in particular, is often on the scene. He's a very sophisticated guy—eats at all the best restaurants around the world. (He also kids Jack about "hiding" me away in the kitchen. . . . I tell him I *like* being in the kitchen, thank you very much.) Anyway, he loves these green beans. The food comes out, and he's first in line. I'm always pleased (and a little amazed) to see that people like him, who are accustomed to three-star restaurant service, can still be so delighted with such a simple, home-cooked dish.

These can be made several hours ahead, but add the vinegar at the last minute. It will dull the bright green color of the beans over time.

BRING A LARGE POT OF WATER to a boil and add salt until the water tastes lightly salted (about ¼ cup). Put a colander in the sink.

Add the beans to the pot, start timing, and cook until tender, 9 to 10 minutes. Drain in the colander.

Dump the beans into a serving bowl. Add the olive oil, parsley, garlic, and salt to taste (I don't use any, but you may like to), and stir gently so that all the beans are coated with the oil. If you are serving the beans immediately, add the vinegar and stir again. Or, set them aside to cool at room temperature. When they are completely cooled and you're ready to serve, add the vinegar and stir again.

ASPARAGUS ALLA PARMIGIANA

SERVES 4

20 STALKS	*medium asparagus*
	Salt
2 TABLESPOONS	*unsalted butter*
	Freshly ground pepper
½ TABLESPOON	*finely grated Parmesan cheese*

Preparing asparagus Piacenza-style means serving it with the local cheese, in this case, Parmesan. Traditionally this simple dish would be eaten at spring, particularly at Easter time. The Parmesan acts as a light seasoning—don't use too much, or it will overpower the delicate taste of the asparagus.

In my family, we're most likely to eat asparagus hot, as a side dish. But it often appears in Italy as an antipasto, and you can serve it the same way. Cook it as in the recipe below, cool it in ice water, drain, and drizzle on the lemony vinaigrette from the recipe for veal cutlets on page 143.

CUT OFF AND DISCARD the bottom third of the asparagus stalks. Cut four 11-inch pieces of kitchen twine. Bundle the asparagus into four groups of five and tie each bundle together, wrapping it a couple of times around the middle with the twine. This makes it easy to put the asparagus into and take it out of the cooking water.

Bring a medium pot of water (about 1½ quarts) to a boil and add 1½ teaspoons salt. Add the asparagus bundles and simmer gently until the stalks are tender enough that a small knife slides in easily, 5 to 7 minutes. Meanwhile, in a small saucepan, melt the butter.

When the asparagus is cooked, use a fork to pick up each bundle by the string and transfer to a cutting board. Cut off the strings with a knife. Pat the asparagus dry. Arrange the stalks in a single layer on a platter and spoon the melted butter all over so that they are all completely coated. Sprinkle with a little more salt and 3 to 5 twists of a pepper grinder. Use a spoon to lightly sprinkle the cheese so that the entirety of each asparagus stalk is lightly but entirely coated. Serve warm.

THE TWIST

The ends of asparagus stalks are too tough and woody to make pleasant eating; they must be trimmed. My mom trims the bottom inch and peels the rest of the stalk (which makes it entirely edible), so as to waste as little as possible. My students are put off by all that peeling, so I teach the easy way: just cut off and discard the bottom third of the stalk.

BAKED CAULIFLOWER

SERVES 6 TO 8

A blanket of besciamella sauce and a sprinkle of Parmesan cheese turn this everyday vegetable into something much more special than you'd expect. Because this is a little rich, it's best served with lean meats such as roast chicken (page 122), veal roast (145), or veal cutlets (page 143).

PULL OFF AND DISCARD the leaves from the cauliflower. Cut the head in half through the stem end, then cut each half in half again through the stem end. Rinse the quarters well under cold running water.

Bring a large pot of water to a boil. Add enough salt to make the water taste salty (about ¼ cup) and the lemon slice. Add the cauliflower quarters. Return the water to a boil and simmer, partially covered, until the stem of the cauliflower is tender when you stick a fork into it, but there's still some resistance, about 15 minutes. (The florets will cook faster; you don't want them turning to mush.) Using a slotted spoon, remove the cauliflower to a colander and drain.

For the besciamella, in a saucepan, melt 4 tablespoons of the butter over medium heat and cook until it bubbles. Remove the pan from the heat. Add the flour and stir well with a wooden spoon to blend; there should be almost no lumps. Return the pan to the heat and stir until completely smooth. Let the mixture bubble for 2 minutes, stirring constantly and making sure to get into the sides of the pan. Add the milk, gradually at first and stirring constantly, until blended, then pour in the rest more quickly. Cook without simmering, stirring constantly until the sauce thickens, 8 to 10 minutes. Remove the pan from the heat. Add the salt, nutmeg, and half of the cheese, and stir until smooth.

Preheat the oven to 350°F and center a rack in the oven. Butter a 9-by-13-inch baking dish. With a fork and knife, lift the cauliflower out of the colander and into the baking dish, cutting it into large florets as you work. Discard the main portion of the stem, if you like, or cut it up and use it. Arrange the cauliflower in a single layer. Spoon the besciamella over. Sprinkle all over, evenly, with the remaining 2 tablespoons cheese. Dot the top with the remaining ½ tablespoon butter, cut into bits. Bake until the top turns golden brown in places, 20 to 25 minutes. (If your oven doesn't brown well, you can brown the cauliflower under the broiler.) Serve hot.

1 HEAD	*cauliflower*
	Salt
1 THICK SLICE	*lemon*
	BESCIAMELLA AND TOPPING
4½ TABLESPOONS	*unsalted butter*
2 TABLESPOONS PLUS 2 TEASPOONS	*all-purpose flour*
2 CUPS	*milk*
½ TEASPOON	*salt*
PINCH	*freshly ground nutmeg*
¼ CUP	*finely grated Parmesan cheese*

BAKED FENNEL

WITH PARMESAN CHEESE AND BUTTER

SERVES 4 TO 6

3	*large fennel bulbs, about 14 ounces each, tops cut off and discarded, bulbs washed and patted dry*
	Salt
4 TABLESPOONS	*unsalted butter*
1 TABLESPOON	*finely grated Parmesan cheese*
	Freshly ground pepper

SHOPPING WITH ANNA

Look for very white (not green) fennel bulbs—they will be the most tender.

This is a nice side dish to serve for a dinner party. It's delicious, and it's five ingredients. Period. It's also a little different (always a plus at a party), and the presentation makes it look like it took more time to make than it really did.

This recipe gives me the chance to address a question I run into with my students a lot . . . *butter*. People tend to be wary of butter. I don't teach this recipe so much because I know people will ask, "Do I *have* to use butter?" or "Can I use olive oil instead?" Well, yes, of course you can! But I guarantee you, butter is exactly the right thing to bring out the delicate flavor of cooked fennel. And it tastes so good with the Parmesan.

It's really a question of balance. I would never recommend a menu in which *everything* was laden with butter, but I love it in a dish or two. So for example, since the recipe calls for 4 tablespoons of butter, don't serve it with a saucy, creamy entrée like paglia e fieno (page 86) or lasagne (page 95). *Do* serve it with a grilled veal chop (page 138), roast chicken (page 122), or branzino in salt (page 112)—something without all the sauce.

REMOVE THE ENTIRE OUTER LAYER of each fennel bulb—it's likely to be tough. Trim the bottoms. Cut the bulbs in half through the core ends, set each half cut side down on the work surface, and cut them half again through the core ends so that you have 12 quarters.

Bring about 1 inch water to a simmer in the bottom of a steamer pot and add salt until the water tastes lightly salted. Place the fennel quarters in the steamer basket, in a single layer, if possible. Set the basket over the boiling water, cover, and steam until the blade of a small knife goes into the bulbs easily, 15 to 25 minutes, depending on the fennel. Set aside until cool enough to handle.

Preheat the oven to 350°F. In a small pot, melt the butter. Arrange the fennel quarters in a single layer in a 9-by-13-inch baking dish, evenly spaced, rounded sides facing down. Spoon the melted butter over, coating each quarter. Sprinkle the fennel with cheese and pepper. Bake 30 minutes.

Preheat the broiler and arrange a rack 4 to 6 inches from the element. Broil the fennel until the cheese and butter turn golden brown, 3 to 5 minutes. Serve hot or at room temperature.

SAUTÉED MUSHROOMS
WITH GARLIC AND PARSLEY

SERVES 4

2 (10-OUNCE) PACKAGES	*baby portobello mushrooms*
5 TABLESPOONS	*extra-virgin olive oil*
	Salt and freshly ground pepper
1 CLOVE	*garlic, finely chopped*
1½ TABLESPOONS	*chopped fresh Italian parsley*

Two packages of mushrooms looks like a lot for four people, but they cook down quite a bit. My dad likes these on hamburgers. I serve them with roasted chicken, grilled veal chops, or fish.

WIPE THE MUSHROOMS with a damp paper towel. Cut off the stems and slice the caps thinly.

Heat the oil in a 10-inch skillet over medium heat. When the pan is hot, add the mushrooms and use your spoon to pat them into an even layer. Turn the heat down to medium-low and cook 6 minutes without stirring. Add 1 teaspoon salt and ¼ teaspoon pepper. Turn the mushrooms with a spoon and continue cooking until they are tender but not browned, 5 to 6 more minutes. The mushrooms will give off some cooking liquid—don't worry about it; the liquid will keep them moist.

Stir in the garlic and cook 3 more minutes. Remove the pan from the heat and stir in the parsley. Serve hot or room temperature.

THE TWIST

A salad spinner is a useful tool that my grandfather and his brothers never had access to. And not just for salads; if you wash and spin it thoroughly dry, parsley will keep for a week—even two —in the refrigerator.

When you bring home a bunch from the supermarket, cut off the thick stems and put the sprigs in the basket of the salad spinner. Fill the bowl with water (or another bowl, if your spinner bowl has a drainage hole); add the basket and let the parsley soak for a few minutes to loosen the sand and grit. Lift out the basket; the grit should stay in the bowl. Replace the gritty water with fresh water and soak the parsley again. Dump the water, and spin the parsley until very dry.

Roll the clean parsley sprigs in a length (3 squares) of paper toweling. Place them in a resealable plastic bag and refrigerate.

ROASTED POTATOES

WITH ROSEMARY

SERVES 4 TO 6

My mom always had rosemary growing in the garden (in the winter it's indoors in a pot on her kitchen windowsill), and one of my early garden duties was to go out and cut a sprig for these rosemary-scented roasted potatoes. Traditionally the potatoes are peeled, but I like to leave the skins on. They're pretty and nutritious. And do I need to say that it's less work *not* to peel?

If you want to get going on the potatoes ahead of time, you can quarter them (peeled or not) and leave them in a bowl of cold water for several hours; the water keeps the potatoes from blackening.

PREHEAT THE OVEN to 400°F.

Peel the potatoes and cut them into quarters. Put them in a 9-by-13-inch baking dish. Pull the needles off the rosemary sprig and sprinkle them over the potatoes. Drizzle with the oil and sprinkle with the salt. Toss so that the potatoes are entirely coated with oil and salt.

Roast the potatoes until they have developed a nicely browned skin and the interiors are meltingly soft, 1 hour to 1 hour 15 minutes. About 40 minutes into the roasting, stir the potatoes for even cooking.

2 TO 2¼ POUNDS	*red potatoes (about 6)*
1 (6-INCH) SPRIG	*fresh rosemary*
¼ CUP	*extra-virgin olive oil*
¾ TEASPOON	*salt*

PEPERONATA

SERVES 4

Cooked slowly with olive oil and onion, bell peppers develop a very differ-ent flavor than when they're roasted—they're sweet! And the capers add a little kick. You can serve these peppers hot or at room temperature. I'll often make them in the middle of the day and leave them at room temperature, covered, to serve with roast chicken or fish at dinnertime. And if we have leftover meat loaf, Jack likes to nab some of the peppers for his meat loaf sandwich.

CUT THE STEMS OFF the peppers. Cut the peppers in half and pull out the seeds. Cut out the white, fleshy ribs with a small knife. Place the pepper halves, cut sides down, on a cutting board and cut them crosswise into strips about ⅓ inch thick. Try to make them a consistent thickness so that they will cook evenly.

Halve the onion through the stem end; place it cut side down on the cutting board and slice it crosswise into strips about the same width as the peppers.

In a 10-inch skillet, heat the oil over low heat. Add the peppers, onion, garlic, 1 teaspoon salt, and ¼ teaspoon pepper. Stir well to coat the vegetables with the oil. Cook slowly, stirring every now and then for even cooking, until the peppers are very soft but not brown, 35 to 40 minutes. Stir in the capers.

2	*firm red bell peppers*
2	*firm yellow bell peppers*
1	*Vidalia (or other sweet) onion*
5 TABLESPOONS	*extra-virgin olive oil*
1 CLOVE	*garlic, finely chopped or pressed through a garlic press*
	Salt and freshly ground pepper
1 TEASPOON	*drained nonpareil capers (the tiny ones)*

BUTTERNUT SQUASH

SERVES 4 TO 6

2 (20-OUNCE) PACKAGES	*cleaned, cubed squash*
2 TABLESPOONS	*extra-virgin olive oil, plus extra for the baking sheet*
	Salt and freshly ground pepper

I love squash. In fact, I prefer it to potatoes. This recipe is super easy—just the squash, a little olive oil and seasonings—so you really taste the vegetable. Anytime one would normally serve roasted potatoes, I make this instead.

You can also make it with kabocha squash (see page 99).

PREHEAT THE OVEN to 400°F. Smear a rimmed baking sheet with olive oil.

Put the cubed squash in a bowl. Add the oil, 1 teaspoon salt, and ¼ teaspoon pepper, and toss with a spoon to coat the squash with the oil.

Spread the squash in a single layer on the baking sheet and roast until a fork penetrates easily but the squash isn't yet falling apart—it should just be beginning to brown, 45 to 55 minutes. (If the squash starts to brown within the first 30 minutes, cover it with a sheet of aluminum foil.) Transfer the squash to a serving bowl and taste for seasoning.

THE TWIST

Round like a pumpkin (though not as tall), green on the outside, and bright orange inside, the Italian squash, called zucca, *is loaded with flavor. Italians use zucca in all sorts of things: roasted, as a side dish (above), pureed into soup (page 45), as a filling for ravioli (page 98), even cut into pieces, boiled, and stirred into rice. I can't get zucca in America so I substitute butternut or kabocha squash. Butternut is sold practically everywhere, and you can buy it cleaned and cubed (very convenient!).*

STUFFED TOMATOES

SERVES 4

This is a summer recipe, at its best when tomatoes are delicious, flavorful, and plentiful. But one of my favorite memories of it was when we made it for Christmas one year. My mom had come across some good-tasting, small tomatoes. We stuffed them and served them on a large, white platter. Against the white, the red looked so nice—Christmas-y and festive.

This is another good party recipe: easy, but fancy looking. It can be multiplied for however many servings you need. Serve the tomatoes hot or within about 30 minutes of taking them out of the oven.

CUT OFF AND DISCARD the tops of the tomatoes. Scoop out the pulp and seeds and set the hollowed tomatoes aside. Chop the pulp, discarding any hard bits, then transfer it to a small bowl.

Place a small metal rack on top of a wide bowl or a medium baking dish. Sprinkle the interiors of the hollowed-out tomatoes with about ½ teaspoon salt (total), and set them upside down on the rack. Let them stand for 1 hour to drain off some of their liquid.

Meanwhile, in a small skillet, heat the oil with the chopped garlic over low heat. Cook very gently to flavor the oil without browning the garlic, about 2 minutes. Add the chopped tomato pulp (reserve the bowl) and let it come to a simmer over low heat. Add the bread crumbs and stir well to blend. Cook 2 minutes. Remove from the heat and scrape the mixture back into the bowl. Add the Parmesan, parsley, basil, and a pinch each salt and pepper. Stir well to blend. The stuffing should be moist but not soupy.

Preheat the oven to 400°F. Oil a pie dish or other baking dish just large enough to hold the tomatoes. With a spoon, mound the stuffing in the tomatoes. Set the tomatoes in the baking dish. Drizzle the top of each with olive oil. Bake until the tomatoes are soft and the stuffing has developed a golden crust, about 40 minutes.

4	plum or other medium-sized tomatoes
	Salt
1 TABLESPOON	extra-virgin olive oil, plus extra for drizzling and oiling the baking dish
½ CLOVE	garlic, very finely chopped
¼ CUP	Italian-style dried bread crumbs
3 TABLESPOONS	finely grated Parmesan
1 TABLESPOON	chopped fresh Italian parsley
2 LEAVES	fresh basil, chopped
	Freshly ground pepper

BUTTERY SPINACH
WITH PARMESAN CHEESE

SERVES 4

20 OUNCES	*spinach, thick stems trimmed, leaves washed and spun dry (fine if some water still clings to the leaves)*
½ TEASPOON	*salt*
3 TABLESPOONS	*unsalted butter*
2 TABLESPOONS	*finely grated Parmesan cheese*

I like to use baby spinach in salads (it's so convenient), but for this dish, adult spinach has more flavor. Serve it with roast chicken (page 122), veal chops (page 138), veal or pork roast (page 145), or branzino (page 112).

HEAT A LARGE SOUP POT over medium-high heat for about 1 minute to get it nice and hot. Add the spinach, pressing it into the pot as needed to make it fit. Add the salt. Cover and cook until the spinach is wilted and the stems are softened, 10 to 12 minutes.

Remove the pot from the heat. Drain the spinach if there's liquid in the pot and return to the pot. Add the butter and cheese and stir well with a wooden spoon to melt the butter.

Nonna Anna (foreground) and my grandfather (background) on a cruise ship bound for Italy.

ZUCCHINI ROUNDS

WITH OIL AND VINEGAR

SERVES 4

A yummy way to serve zucchini. Try not to stir the rounds too much while they're cooking, or they'll fall apart. Balsamic vinegar gives the dish a little sweetness, but it's not mandatory—my grandmother never cooked with it. My mom and I both like it, so we use it here.

TRIM THE TOPS and ends from the zucchini. Cut the zucchini into ⅓-inch-thick rounds. Place them in a colander, toss with the salt, and set the colander on a deep plate to catch the liquid. Cover with a piece of paper towel and set a heavy can on top to help press the liquid out of the zucchini. Let stand at room temperature at least 1 hour, or up to 4 hours. Spread the zucchini slices out on a paper towel and pat them dry.

Heat the oil in a 10-inch skillet over medium-low heat. When the pan is hot, add the zucchini slices, spreading them out over the bottom of the pan, and let them cook without browning for 10 minutes. Then carefully turn the zucchini with a spoon or spatula and cook until soft, about 10 more minutes. If they begin to brown, turn down the heat.

Gently stir in the parsley, garlic powder, and balsamic vinegar, if using. Serve hot or at room temperature.

4	*firm zucchini (about 1½ pounds total)*
1 TEASPOON	*salt*
2½ TABLESPOONS	*extra-virgin olive oil*
1 TABLESPOON	*chopped fresh Italian parsley*
¼ TEASPOON	*garlic powder (not garlic salt!)*
¼ TEASPOON	*balsamic vinegar (optional)*

STUFFED ZUCCHINI BOATS

SERVES 4

3	firm zucchini (about 1¼ pounds), trimmed and washed
	Salt
1½ TABLESPOONS	extra-virgin olive oil, plus extra for drizzling
¼	onion, finely chopped (about 2 tablespoons)
1 CLOVE	garlic, minced
	Freshly ground pepper
½ CUP	plain, dried bread crumbs
1½ TABLESPOONS	chopped fresh Italian parsley
1	thin slice boiled ham, finely chopped (about 3 tablespoons)
1 TABLESPOON	finely grated pecorino cheese
1 TABLESPOON	finely grated Parmesan cheese
1	large egg
1 TABLESPOON	unsalted butter, plus extra for the baking dish

We stuff zucchini in the summertime when squash is at its best. The stuffing is made with bread crumbs and is similar to the mixture we use for stuffing tomatoes, but with a little ham and pecorino cheese added. For a fancier occasion, you can replace the bread crumbs with besciamella. Serve these with roast chicken or capon (page 122 or 119), or a veal roast (page 145). This is a nice dish for a party buffet because it looks pretty and is tasty at room temperature.

CUT THE ZUCCHINI in half lengthwise and scoop out the insides with a melon baller (leaving the sides of the "boats" about ¼ inch thick). Place the scoopings on a cutting board and coarsely chop them.

Choose a baking dish large enough to hold the zucchini boats in a single layer and rub it with butter. Bring a large pot of water to a boil and add 1 tablespoon salt. Set a colander in a baking dish next to the stove. Add the zucchini boats and boil 4 minutes, until they are about halfway cooked. Remove with a spider or slotted spoon to the colander and drain. Place the zucchini in a single layer in the prepared baking dish.

Preheat the oven to 375°F.

For the stuffing, in a small saucepan, heat the 1½ tablespoons oil over low heat. Add the onion and cook until softened, 7 to 8 minutes. Add the chopped zucchini and stir. Increase the heat to medium and cook until tender, about 5 minutes. (Turn the heat down if the mixture begins to brown.) Add the garlic, stir well, and cook 2 minutes. Stir in ¼ teaspoon salt and ⅛ teaspoon pepper. Add the bread crumbs and stir well.

Spoon the stuffing into a medium bowl and stir in the parsley, ham, and cheeses. In a small bowl, beat the egg with a fork until blended. Add it to the stuffing and stir until it's completely incorporated.

Spoon the stuffing into the zucchini shells. Drizzle with a little more olive oil, and cut the butter into small pieces to dot the mounds of stuffing. Bake until the stuffing has developed a golden crust, about 35 minutes.

MIXED SALAD

SERVES 4

1 CLOVE	*garlic, mashed with the heel of your hand and peeled*
2 CUPS	*mixed, torn, red leaf lettuce and hearts of escarole, washed and dried*
2 CUPS	*arugula, washed and dried*
½ HEAD	*radicchio*
1	*ripe tomato*
1 TABLESPOON	*extra-virgin olive oil*
	Freshly ground pepper
VINAIGRETTE	
1 TABLESPOON	*vinegar*
½ TEASPOON	*salt*
⅛ TEASPOON	*freshly ground pepper*
¼ CUP	*extra-virgin olive oil*

ABOUT YOUR KITCHEN STUFF

A salad spinner makes it easy to have clean lettuce in the refrigerator all the time. I buy several heads at once. Working in batches, put the lettuce leaves in the basket of the salad spinner. Fill the bowl of the spinner with cold water; add the basket and let the lettuce soak for a few minutes. Lift out the basket; the grit will stay in the bowl. Dump the water, refill with fresh water, and soak the lettuce again. Dump.

An Italian mixed salad generally means a mixture of lettuces and tomatoes. But in Italy, we give the tomatoes special treatment. There, tomatoes are usually picked ripe from local farms. (They're not mass-produced into having zero flavor, as they often are here in the United States.) They have a nicely balanced acidity, and we don't like to overpower that with vinegar. So we slice the tomatoes and drizzle them with olive oil. The lettuces are dressed separately with a vinaigrette. When it's time to eat, the dressed greens are spooned onto serving plates, and the tomato slices go on top.

The greens are dressed with my go-to vinaigrette: 1 part vinegar to 4 parts oil. You can make it in any quantity, with any vinegar (balsamic, red, or white wine vinegar)—the proportions remain the same. And the salad is scented with a hint of garlic, rubbed over the inside of the salad bowl.

RUB THE INSIDE of a salad bowl with the cut side of the garlic and discard the garlic. Add the red leaf lettuce, escarole, and arugula. Slice the radicchio very thin and add it to the bowl.

Core the tomato, cut it in quarters, and slice the quarters about ½-inch thick. Place the tomato slices on a plate. Drizzle them with the oil, and sprinkle with a pinch of pepper.

To make the vinaigrette, put the vinegar in a small bowl. Add the salt and pepper and whisk to dissolve the salt. Whisk in the oil.

To serve, pour the vinaigrette over the lettuces and toss well. Spoon the tomatoes on top.

TOMATO, GREEN PEPPER, AND RED ONION SALAD

SERVES 4

We make this summer salad with at least two kinds of tomatoes: plum and beefsteak, to take advantage of the difference in flavor and texture between the two. And if I see a yellow tomato at the market, I also throw that in, for color. Just like all of our tomato salads, there's no vinegar in this one. Just oil and lots of salt to bring out the flavor of the tomatoes.

CUT THE TOMATOES into 1-inch chunks and put them in a serving bowl.

Stand the bell pepper on end and cut the pepper off the core in large pieces with a large knife. Cut the pepper into thin slices, and cut the slices in half. Put the sliced pepper in the bowl with the tomatoes.

Cut the onion into thin slices and add it to the bowl. Sprinkle with the salt and pepper, and add the oil. Toss well and serve.

3	ripe plum tomatoes, stemmed
2	ripe beefsteak tomatoes, stemmed
1	green bell pepper
⅓	large red onion
½ TABLESPOON	salt
⅛ TEASPOON	freshly ground pepper
5 TABLESPOONS	extra-virgin olive oil

GRATED CARROT SALAD

SERVES 4 TO 6

I POUND	*carrots, peeled*
I TABLESPOON	*fresh lemon juice*
½ TEASPOON	*salt*
⅛ TEASPOON	*freshly ground pepper*
3 TABLESPOONS	*extra-virgin olive oil*
	KITCHEN STUFF
	A food processor with a blade for coarse grating

The way to survive cooking a big dinner party is to be smart about the menu. I'm constantly on the lookout for easy-to-make dishes that add color and variety to the buffet table, and that offset the work of more time-consuming recipes. This one fits the bill perfectly! It's become a standard at Jack's birthday dinners because it's light and refreshing (great for a July birthday) and easy to make in volume.

But don't wait for a party to make the salad. It works just as well for a casual dinner, and it's saved my life a number of times when I ran out of lettuce.

GRATE THE CARROTS on the large hole of a grater or better still, if you have one, in a food processor. Put them in a serving bowl.

To make the vinaigrette, put the lemon juice in a small bowl. Add the salt and pepper and whisk to dissolve the salt. Whisk in the oil. Pour the dressing over the carrots and stir well. That's it.

WINTERTIME FENNEL AND RADISH SALAD

SERVES 4 TO 6

Many of my students think they don't like fennel, a mildly licorice-tasting, celery-like vegetable that we adore in Italy. This crunchy, fresh-tasting salad usually changes their minds. But I tell them to be sure to make it only during the winter months. Although you'll find it in supermarkets year round, fennel is at its best from fall through early spring, when its color is more white than green. Out of season, it can be unpleasantly tough.

We sometimes top off the salad with shaved Parmesan. If you'd like to do that, use a vegetable peeler or the coarse holes of grater to cut thin shards.

3	*fennel bulbs*
5	*large radishes*
3 TABLESPOONS	*extra-virgin olive oil*
¾ TEASPOON	*salt*
⅛ TEASPOON	*freshly ground pepper*

TRIM THE STALKS from the fennel all the way down to the bulbs and discard them, and cut a thin sliver off the bulb ends. Cut the bulbs in half through the stem ends and cut out the triangular white cores. (This step is optional, but the core is a little tough.) Lay the fennel halves, flat side down, on the cutting board, and thinly slice them crosswise. Put the sliced fennel in a bowl.

Trim the tops off the radishes, and thinly slice them crosswise; add them to the bowl. Add the oil, salt, and pepper, and toss.

FENNEL FACTS

In Italy, we're taught that there are two types of fennel: male and female. The female bulbs have a rounded shape (they have hips!) while the male bulbs are flatter, and more slender. The slender bulbs are tougher, so I buy the ladies.

NIÇOISE SALAD

3	*large red-skinned potatoes*
¼ TEASPOON	*Dijon mustard*
⅛ TEASPOON	*salt*
¼ CUP	*white wine vinegar*
½ CUP	*extra-virgin olive oil*
½ POUND	*green beans, ends trimmed*
3	*large eggs*
I SMALL HEAD	*Bibb lettuce, washed, dried, and torn into bite-sized pieces*
4	*large plum tomatoes, stem ends trimmed, cut into 1- to 1½-inch chunks*
7 OUNCES	*tuna (preferably imported) packed in olive oil, broken into bite-sized chunks*
½ CUP	*black olives, preferably Niçoise*

This salad is typical of the northern regions of Italy, near France. An easy, fresh summer entrée salad, it's great for a picnic: Bibb lettuce layered with green beans, red potatoes, Italian canned tuna, tomatoes, and black olives, then dressed with a mustardy vinaigrette.

The salad is put together in layers, almost like a lasagne. We serve it in a glass baking dish, so that you can see the layers with all the different colors. You can use any black olive you like; the small Niçoise olives are traditional and very good.

The potatoes are dressed while they're still warm so that they absorb the oil and vinegar. And the oil and vinegar will seep into and flavor the lettuce and tomato, too.

PUT THE POTATOES in a saucepan and add cold water to cover. Bring to a boil, reduce the heat, cover, and simmer the potatoes until they are tender when pierced with a small knife, 25 to 30 minutes. Drain the potatoes, and let sit until cool enough to handle, about 10 minutes. While they are still warm, peel them with a small knife. Cut the potatoes into 1½-inch cubes (quarter them lengthwise and then cut the quarters into 1½-inch-wide pieces). In a medium bowl, whisk together the mustard, salt, and vinegar until the salt dissolves. Add the warm potatoes and toss; let that sit for a few minutes. Then add the olive oil and toss to mix; set aside.

Bring another large saucepan of water to a boil. Add the beans and simmer 10 minutes. Drain. Refrigerate the beans until chilled, then cut them in half.

Put the eggs in a saucepan and add cold water to cover. Bring them to a boil over medium-high heat. Reduce the heat and simmer 8 minutes. Cool the eggs under cold, running water and peel.

To assemble the salad, arrange the lettuce over the bottom of a 9-by-13-inch glass baking dish. Spoon the potatoes in a layer on top of the lettuce, drizzling them with any of the oil and vinegar left in the bowl. Arrange the tomatoes over the potatoes. Arrange the tuna chunks over the tomatoes. Cut the eggs in half lengthwise, and then slice them into chunks; layer the chunks over the tuna. Sprinkle the salad with the beans and then the olives.

FOR THE VINAIGRETTE, whisk together the mustard, salt, pepper, and vinegar until the salt dissolves. Then whisk in the oil, pouring it gradually from the measuring cup and whisking all the time, so that it thickens. (This works great in a food processor too; add the oil through the feed tube with the motor running.)

Drizzle the vinaigrette over the salad. Let stand for a few minutes (or up to 30 minutes) before serving.

	MUSTARDY VINAIGRETTE
¼ TEASPOON	Dijon mustard
¼ TEASPOON	salt
⅛ TEASPOON	freshly ground pepper
2 TABLESPOONS	red or white wine vinegar
½ CUP	extra-virgin olive oil

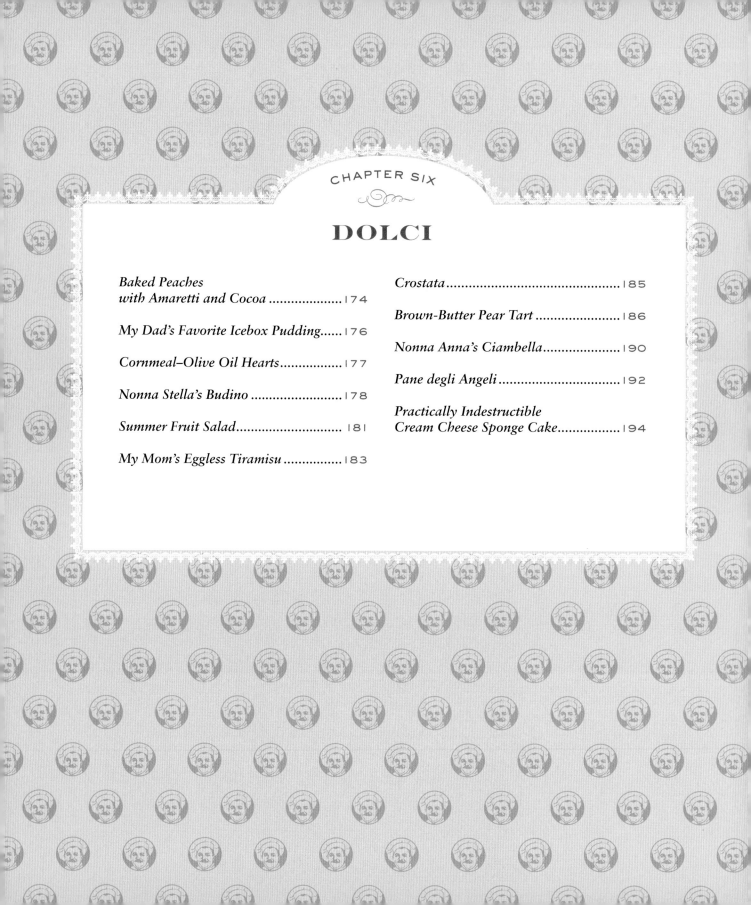

CHAPTER SIX

DOLCI

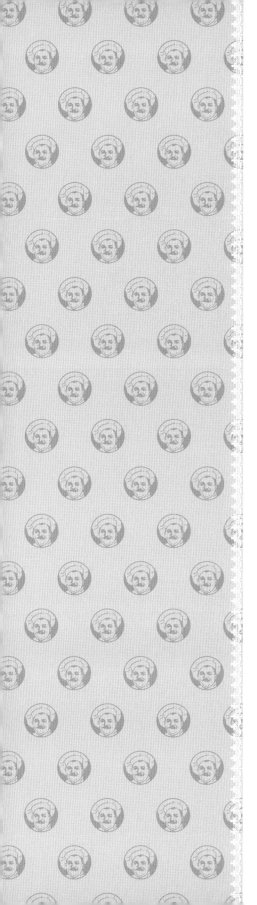

Italian desserts are typically fairly minimal. In the summer, we eat a lot of fruit in salads, tarts, and baked dishes. The cakes are traditionally light and dry, the better to dunk in coffee or a sweet wine. The Boiardi brothers weren't bakers, but my grandmothers were; I learned to make many of these desserts from Nonna Anna and Nonna Stella. Others, my mom and I concocted more recently. One, I learned from my dad (*there's* a hilarious story).

Some of these recipes will require a trip to a specialty cookware store for equipment: the Brown-Butter Pear Tart and the Crostata both need a 9-inch fluted tart pan with a removable bottom. For the Ciambella, you'll need a 10-inch Bundt pan. Both the Pane degli Angeli and the Cream Cheese Sponge Cake call for a 9-inch springform pan, and you'll need 3½-inch soufflé molds for Nonna Stella's Budino.

And while the Cornmeal-Olive Oil Hearts will *taste* just as good if you cut them out with a glass, they'll look very sweet if you find yourself a heart-shaped cookie cutter.

Here is a chapter full of the family's favorite cakes, cookies, puddings, tarts, and fruit desserts to serve at the end of the meal or as an afternoon snack.

BAKED PEACHES

WITH AMARETTI AND COCOA

SERVES 4

	Unsalted butter, for the baking dish
4	*ripe peaches, washed and patted dry*
5 TABLESPOONS	*crushed amaretti cookies (about 2 ounces)*
1	*large egg yolk*
½ TEASPOON	*cocoa powder*
¼ CUP	*dry white wine, such as Pinot Grigio*
	Whipped cream, for serving (optional, see page 184)

SHOPPING WITH ANNA

To hurry along not-very-ripe peaches, put them in a paper bag, close the top, and let them sit at room temperature until they ripen. I wish I could give you a specific length of time, but you just need to keep checking until they're ready.

Peaches are abundant in the area around Piacenza. My mom's mother, Nonna Stella, used to use them in this traditional dish during the months when the peaches were at their best. In fact, my mom likes to tell me how, when she was pregnant, she ate them nonstop.

The peaches should be very ripe and juicy. If they're not so juicy, you may need to chop an extra peach half for the filling, to add a little moisture. Make amaretti crumbs by pulsing the cookies in a food processor, or putting them in a resealable plastic bag, and crushing them with a rolling pin or a meat mallet.

BUTTER A BAKING DISH large enough to hold 8 peach halves in a single layer.

Cut the peaches in half with a small knife and remove the pits. Cut off the peel in strips. Place the peach halves in the baking dish as you finish peeling them.

Use a melon baller to scoop out some of the center pulp from each peach, being careful not to perforate the edges, to make little containers for the filling. Put the peach pulp on a cutting board and finely chop it; transfer it to a small bowl. Add the cookie crumbs, the egg yolk, and the cocoa powder, and stir to combine.

Preheat the oven to 350°F and center a rack in the oven.

Divide the filling among the peach halves. Pour the wine into the dish around the peaches. Bake 30 to 35 minutes or until a thin crust forms on the filling. Let cool to room temperature or refrigerate until chilled. Serve with whipped cream, if you like.

ICEBOX PUDDING

SERVES 8

18	*rectangular graham crackers (36 squares)*
2 (2.75-OUNCE) BOXES	*chocolate pudding (not instant)*
4 CUPS	*whole milk*

This is one of my dad's favorite desserts. I don't make it for anyone but him; it doesn't live anywhere else in my life.

My grandmother used to make it for him. One day—I guess she wasn't around—he said, "I'd really like to have an icebox cake. Why don't you learn to make it?" I was probably nine years old. I'd never made pudding before, but it was my dad, so I said, "Oh, sure!"

So, we're in the kitchen. I put the milk and the chocolate pudding mix into the saucepan, and the pan goes on the heat. I have no idea what I'm doing. My dad's helping, but his directions are a little sketchy, and he's thrown away the box with the directions. I make the pudding, and then I make the cake, and it is all very fun.

But when we are eating it together later, I say, "Doesn't this taste kind of funny? It has kind of a . . . smoky taste."

"Oh, no," he says.

He didn't have the heart to tell me that the pudding was completely, *horribly* scorched. (I didn't know that I had to stir the pudding while it was heating.) He ate it anyway, at least in front of me. So make sure to stir while the pan is on the heat. I guarantee, nothing else can possibly go wrong.

You'll need to buy a 14.4-ounce box of graham crackers; you'll use about two-thirds of the box.

COVER THE BOTTOM of an 8-inch square glass baking dish with a single layer of graham crackers, breaking and piecing the crackers to fit.

In a saucepan, make both packages of pudding with the 4 cups milk (2 cups per package) according to the package directions, making sure to stir as it comes to a simmer. Remove the pan from the heat.

Spread about one-quarter of the pudding over the graham crackers, covering the crackers completely.

Make another layer of graham crackers and spread with another quarter of the pudding. Continue this process until you've used all the pudding and crackers, ending with a layer of pudding. Cover and refrigerate until completely chilled, several hours or overnight. Super, super simple!

CORNMEAL–OLIVE OIL HEARTS

MAKES ABOUT 40 COOKIES

This is a mother-daughter, gluten-free concoction inspired by the gluten-free pane degli angeli (on page 192), which is also made with olive oil. A combination of potato starch, rice flour, and very fine cornmeal makes the cookies light and crisp, and they're not too sweet. You don't need to make them in heart shapes—cut them into any shape you like—but the hearts are particularly sweet.

For a professional look, when the cookies have cooled completely, melt 4 ounces semisweet chocolate in a double boiler. Dip the bottom half of the finished cookies in the warm chocolate; set them on parchment paper to dry.

Don't use extra-virgin olive oil in this recipe—the flavor is too strong. Use one labeled simply "olive oil" or "pure olive oil."

STIR TOGETHER all the dry ingredients in a large bowl. In a second bowl, whisk together the oil and 1 of the eggs. Whisk the second egg in a measuring cup to blend; add half to the bowl and discard the other half.

Make a well in the dry ingredients and pour the olive oil mixture into the center. Use a fork to draw the dry ingredients into the center, stirring, until the mixture gets too stiff to work with the fork. Then mash and knead with clean hands to make a smooth dough.

Dust a work surface with a little rice flour. Place the dough on the board and shape it into a 5-inch square. Wrap it in plastic and chill for 30 minutes.

Preheat the oven to 350°F. Dust the work surface again with rice flour. Line a baking sheet with parchment paper. Roll the dough about ¼ inch thick and cut out 1½- to 2-inch hearts with a heart-shaped cookie cutter. Place the hearts on the prepared baking sheet. Press the dough scraps together, reroll them, and cut out more cookies. Keep rolling and cutting until you've used all the dough.

Bake until the cookies are lightly browned and crisp, 17 to 20 minutes. Let cool on a wire rack.

1 CUP	rice flour, plus extra for dusting
½ CUP	very fine cornmeal
½ CUP	potato starch
½ CUP PLUS 2 TABLESPOONS	confectioners' sugar
2¼ TEASPOONS	baking powder
¼ CUP	olive oil
2	large eggs (of which you'll use only 1½)
	A few drops pure vanilla extract

KITCHEN STUFF

	Heart-shaped or other cookie cutter
	Parchment paper

THE TWIST

To come up with these cookies, my mom and I "twisted" a recipe we got from my aunt. A very good and health-conscious baker, she makes a tapioca-flour cookie that we adjusted for cornmeal and potato starch.

NONNA STELLA'S BUDINO

SERVES 4 TO 6

7 TABLESPOONS PLUS 1 TEASPOON	*all-purpose flour*
½ CUP	*sugar*
1 QUART	*milk*
2 LARGE	*egg yolks*
2 STRIPS	*lemon peel, stripped off with a vegetable peeler*
4 TABLESPOONS (½ STICK)	*unsalted butter, plus extra for buttering the mold*
1 TEASPOON	*pure vanilla extract*
3½ TABLESPOONS	*unsweetened cocoa powder*

This pudding was my Nonna Stella's specialty, and she made it religiously for my brother and me when we visited her in Piacenza. A two-layered concoction of chocolate and vanilla, it was our hands-down favorite dessert. Nonna Stella made it for us in a metal mold (like a Jell-O mold) lined with amaretti cookies that had been soaked in milk. (Brandy and amaretto liqueur are also traditional for soaking, but it was milk for my brother and me.) The two of us used to make such a fuss about who got to eat the most that she switched to individual soufflé dishes so that we could keep track of exactly who had eaten exactly how much. My poor grandmother—we used to drive her crazy.

If we had the patience, she turned the puddings out of the molds before serving, but more often than not, we couldn't wait and ate them straight out of the containers.

Nonna Stella used to stand at the stove, both saucepans going at the same time, stirring the vanilla pudding with one hand and the chocolate with the other. It's easier to make them one at a time. And I don't bother with the cookies.

BUTTER ONE 6-CUP MOLD or eight 3½-inch individual soufflé molds. In each of two medium saucepans, measure 3 tablespoons plus 2 teaspoons of the flour, and ¼ cup sugar. Add 2 cups milk to each pan and whisk well. Place the egg yolks in a small heatproof bowl; set aside.

Place one saucepan over medium heat and bring it to a boil, whisking constantly so that the flour doesn't burn on the bottom of the pan. Remove the pan from the heat. Add a spoonful of the hot mixture to the bowl with the egg yolks and whisk to blend. Pour in the rest of the hot mixture and whisk. Return the mixture to the saucepan, add the lemon strips, and simmer gently, whisking constantly, 7 minutes. Add 2 tablespoons of the butter and cook, whisking, 3 more minutes. Whisk in the vanilla. Pour the pudding into the large buttered mold and smooth it with a spatula or divide it among the small molds, and tap each gently on a work surface to level.

Set the other saucepan over medium heat and bring it to a boil, whisking constantly. Add the cocoa powder, reduce the heat, and simmer gently, whisking constantly, 7 minutes. Add the remaining 2 tablespoons butter and cook,

whisking, 3 more minutes. Pour the chocolate custard over the vanilla custard in the large mold or the small ones and smooth with a spatula.

Cover and refrigerate the pudding until completely set, at least 2 hours. To unmold, overturn a plate on top of the mold. Holding the mold in one hand, and keeping your other hand over the plate, overturn both in one quick movement. The pudding should slide out easily onto the plate.

BUDINO WITH AMARETTI

To make the puddings the way my grandmother used to, pour some brandy, amaretto liqueur, or milk into a bowl. Using one amaretti cookie per mold (if you're using individual molds), quickly roll each cookie twice in the liquid—from one side over to the other side, and then over again— so that the cookies soak up the liquid but don't lose their shape. (They're not supposed to be crunchy; you want them soft, like dry cereal when milk has been poured on it.)

Center one soaked cookie, rounded side down, on the bottom of each mold. Pour the pudding mixture over and chill.

SUMMER FRUIT SALAD

SERVES 2

In the summertime, on restaurant menus all over Italy, you'll always see a version of fruit salad, which we call *macedonia*, sweetened with sugar and lemon. Sometimes it'll be made with melon, sometimes grapes, plums . . . whatever is ripe and locally available. A mix of sliced strawberries and bananas is typical.

This recipe is easy to multiply to serve as many people as you find sitting at your table.

I PINT	*strawberries*
I	*ripe (but not too soft) banana*
2 TABLESPOONS	*sugar*
I TABLESPOON	*fresh lemon juice*

CUT THE TOPS OFF the strawberries and put them in a bowl of cold water. Jounce them around for a couple of seconds; remove and pat dry on paper towels. Slice the strawberries and put them in a serving bowl. Slice the bananas on top.

In a small bowl, whisk together the sugar and lemon juice. Pour over the fruit and toss gently with a spoon.

EGGLESS TIRAMISU

SERVES 12

America is long past its original infatuation with this coffee-flavored sweet, but Italians continue to love it, and so do my students. The name means "pick-me-up"—in Italy, we say that eating tiramisu gives you energy.

The traditional version is made with a creamy mascarpone cheese cream made with raw or lightly cooked egg and layered with a type of Italian lady-finger cookies called *savoiardi* that have been soaked in espresso. My mom, who has an aversion to raw egg, came up with this twist on the original many years ago, substituting chocolate and vanilla puddings for the mascarpone cream.

The whipped cream is optional, but I usually serve a dollop on the side. My meticulous mother uses a piping bag and ruler to draw lines of whipped cream, first all around the edge of the pan, then down the center, and then crosswise to mark off twelve, precisely even, pieces.

GET YOURSELF SET UP with an 8 ¼-by-11½-inch baking dish (preferably Pyrex) and the ladyfingers. You'll use 15 ladyfingers per layer. Pour the coffee into a wide, shallow bowl or an 8-inch square baking dish.

In a saucepan, make the chocolate pudding with 2 cups of the milk according to the package instructions. Set it aside off the heat. Place a ladyfinger in the bowl or baking dish with the coffee and, working quickly so that it doesn't absorb too much coffee, roll the ladyfinger twice in the coffee: from one side over to the other side, and then over again. Place the soaked ladyfinger along one long side of the dish. Roll another ladyfinger in the coffee and place it next to the first. Continue soaking the ladyfingers in the coffee and arranging them in the pan until you have 2 rows of 6 ladyfingers and only the very end of the baking dish has not been filled. Soak 2 more ladyfingers and lay them next to, but perpendicular to the others, the short ends of the cookies flush with one long side of the baking dish. There will just be one corner of the dish empty; cut one last ladyfinger in half widthwise, soak it, and use the halves to fill the dish.

Pour the hot chocolate pudding into the baking dish and smooth it with a rubber spatula to completely cover the ladyfingers.

30	*Italian ladyfingers (savoiardi)*
4 CUPS	*cold coffee*
1 (2.75-OUNCE) BOX	*chocolate pudding (not instant)*
1 QUART	*whole milk*
1 (2.75-OUNCE) BOX	*vanilla pudding (not instant)*
	Cocoa powder
1 CUP	*heavy cream (optional)*
1 TABLESPOON	*confectioners' sugar (optional)*
	KITCHEN STUFF
	Pastry bag fitted with a star tip (optional)
	Fine sieve or sugar shaker

Wash and dry the saucepan. Make the vanilla pudding in the pan with the remaining 2 cups milk according to the package instructions and set it aside. Roll the remaining 15 ladyfingers in the coffee and arrange them precisely as you did before, placing them on top of the chocolate pudding. Pour the hot vanilla pudding over the ladyfingers and smooth it with a rubber spatula. Cover the tiramisu with plastic and refrigerate until it is completely chilled, at least 2 hours or overnight.

Sprinkle the top of the tiramisu lightly and evenly with cocoa powder until the pudding is completely covered (I use a metal sugar shaker, but a fine sieve works too). Stick toothpicks into the tiramisu at 3-inch intervals all around the edges and put three toothpicks down the center. Loosely cover the dessert with a sheet of plastic wrap; the toothpicks will keep the plastic from marring the surface.

Just before serving, combine the cream and sugar in a bowl and whip with an electric mixer or a wire whisk until the cream thickens to stiff peaks. Cut the tiramisu into squares and serve the whipped cream on the side. Or spoon the cream into a pastry bag fitted with a star tip. Decorate all around the edges of the pudding with rosettes of whipped cream. Make a line of rosettes crosswise through the center; draw three more lines, lengthwise, to make twelve even pieces. Cut along the lines to serve.

CROSTATA

A crostata is a sweet, crisp, buttery crust spread with fruit, baked, and dusted with powdered sugar. This is best made the day before you plan to serve it. No need to refrigerate it; just cover and leave it out at room temperature.

IN A FOOD PROCESSOR, combine flour, sugar, salt, and baking powder, and process to combine. Add the butter and pulse until it is cut into the dry ingredients, in pea-sized pieces. In a small bowl, whisk together the whole egg, egg yolk, and vanilla. With the food processor running, pour the egg mixture in through the feed tube and process until the dough forms a ball.

Preheat the oven to 350°F and arrange a rack in the center of the oven. Lightly flour a work surface. Butter a 9-inch fluted tart pan with a removable bottom.

Place the dough on the floured work surface, and cut it in half. Set one half of the dough aside, covered with plastic. Roll the other half into an 11- to 12-inch circle about ⅛ inch thick. Holding the rolling pin at the top of the circle, gently roll the top of the dough around the pin, and then roll the pin toward the bottom of the dough circle until the dough is loosely wrapped around the rolling pin. Position the rolling pin over the tart pan and unroll the dough so that it falls into the pan. Press the dough over the bottom and up the sides of the pan. Don't worry if it breaks; just press the dough together and patch where necessary. Roll the rolling pin over the top of the tart pan to cut off the excess dough. Spread the preserves over the bottom of the tart shell.

Roll the rest of the dough into a rough rectangle ⅛ inch thick. Cut into ½-inch-wide strips using a fluted pastry cutter. Lay the strips across the top of the tart about ½ inch apart. Lay more pastry strips across, positioning them perpendicular to the first layer, and also about ½ inch apart, to make a lattice design. Roll the rolling pin again over the top of the tart to cut off the excess dough.

Bake the crostata until the pastry is golden brown, about 1 hour. Let cool completely on a wire rack. Then set the crostata, in the pan, on top of a large can so that the side of the pan drops off. Place the crostata (don't remove the bottom) on a work surface. Use a fine sieve or sugar shaker to dust it all over with confectioners' sugar. Cut into wedges to serve.

CROSTATA DOUGH

2¼ CUPS	all-purpose flour
¼ CUP	sugar
½ TEASPOON	salt
¼ TEASPOON	baking powder
1 CUP (2 STICKS)	cold, unsalted butter, cut into pieces, plus extra for the pan
1	large egg
1	large egg yolk
1½ TEASPOONS	pure vanilla extract
1 (13-OUNCE) JAR	good-quality raspberry, peach, or apricot preserves
	Confectioners' sugar, for sprinkling

KITCHEN STUFF

9-inch fluted removable-bottomed tart pan

Fine sieve or sugar shaker

Rolling pin

Fluted pastry cutter

BROWN-BUTTER PEAR TART

SERVES 8

SWEET PIE DOUGH

1 ¼ CUPS	all-purpose flour
¼ CUP	sugar
11 TABLESPOONS	cold, unsalted butter
2	large egg yolks
½ TEASPOON	pure vanilla extract
¼ TEASPOON	water

FILLING

½ CUP (1 STICK)	unsalted butter
¾ CUP	sugar
5 TABLESPOONS	all-purpose flour
2	large eggs
3	ripe Bartlett pears

	Confectioners' sugar, for sprinkling

KITCHEN STUFF

	9-inch fluted removable-bottomed tart pan
	Fine sieve or sugar shaker, for dusting
	Rolling pin

My mom developed this tart sometime in the 1980s from a family recipe that she improved upon (she adores doing that). It has a little bit of the feel of a French tart. It's not surprising that my mother has a propensity for French cooking—her great-grandmother grew up outside of Paris.

But fruit tarts are also *very* Italian. When you walk into an Italian bakery, you don't see cupcakes; you see fruit desserts. My mom's family had six different fruit trees in their backyard garden—fig, apricot, plum, pear, apple, and peach—and Nonna Stella made tarts from all of them. This one is so delicious that whenever the family is invited somewhere and we ask what to bring, the answer is always "Oh, bring that wonderful pear tart!"

For such a fabulous thing, it's not so hard to make. The dough is wonderfully rich, like a shortbread cookie. If you have trouble rolling it out, don't worry; you can easily patch it or, worst-case scenario, just press the dough into the pan. You'll have extra dough: just roll and make it into cookies—use cookie cutters, cut squares or triangles with a knife freehand, or make "wreaths" by rolling pieces of dough into ropes about the thickness of a finger and pressing the ends together. Bake them on a buttered baking sheet at 375°F until lightly browned and crisp, about 10 minutes.

You'll need ripe, but still firm, Bartlett pears. (Make sure one of them has a pretty looking stem attached; you'll use just the top third of that one for decoration.) The best way to ensure that they are perfect is to buy them underripe (they generally are anyway), and keep them in a closed paper (not plastic) bag for three to five days at room temperature.

This is actually better the next day. You can leave the uncut tart out overnight, but leftovers should go into the refrigerator the next day.

SET A CUTTING BOARD on your work surface. Butter a 9-inch, fluted tart pan with a removable bottom. Combine the flour and sugar in the bowl of a food processor and process about 10 seconds to combine. Remove the lid and, with a small knife, cut the butter into pieces and into the bowl. Pulse for 45 seconds until the butter is cut into the dry ingredients, in pea-sized pieces.

In a small bowl, whisk together the egg yolks, vanilla, and water (you can use a fork in place of the whisk). With the food processor running, slowly pour the egg mixture through the feed tube and process until the dough forms a ball.

Scrape the dough out onto the cutting board and shape it into a disk. Wrap it in plastic and refrigerate for 20 minutes.

Place the chilled dough on the work surface and roll it into a circle about ⅛ inch thick. Set your tart pan nearby. Gently place the rolling pin at the top of the circle, roll the top of the dough around the pin, and then roll the pin toward the bottom of the dough circle until all of the dough is loosely wrapped around the pin. Holding the rolling pin over the pan, unroll the dough so that it falls into place, then press it into the bottom and up the sides. Don't worry if it tears; just press and patch where necessary. (And if all else fails and the dough falls into pieces, just press the dough, piece by broken piece, into the pan.) Press down all around the sides of the pan to break off the excess (you'll have a lot of extra). Refrigerate the tart shell while you make the filling.

Preheat the oven to 375°F. For the filling, melt the butter in a small saucepan over low heat until it turns a rich, golden brown, and smells nutty. The milk solids will sink to the bottom and turn into dark brown bits; watch carefully so that the solids don't burn. Remove the pan from the heat and set it aside to cool. Meanwhile, combine the sugar and flour in a small bowl and stir together with a fork. Crack the eggs into the bowl and continue stirring until the mixture is very smooth. Set aside.

Cut two of the pears into quarters. Cut out the core from each quarter with a small knife, and then peel each quarter with the knife or a vegetable peeler. Place the pear quarters on the cutting board, rounded side up. Score the quarters crosswise, cutting about halfway through the flesh and making the cuts very close to one another. (Scoring allows the filling to soak into the flesh of the pear.) Arrange the pear quarters in the pie shell like the spokes of a wheel, with the wider ends at the outside edge and the narrow ends pointing toward the center. Once all the pear quarters have been arranged in the pie shell, you should have a round, empty space in the center. Cut off the top 2 inches of the third pear, including the stem. Peel it, score it horizontally in circles, and place it in the center with the stem sticking up.

With a whisk, gradually whisk the cooled brown butter (including all the browned bits on the bottom) into the rest of the filling mixture, until very smooth. Pour the filling all over the pears so that they are entirely coated (they'll stick out) and the spaces between the pears are evenly filled. Bake until the filling puffs and turns a nut-brown color, 60 to 65 minutes. Remove the tart from the oven and cool it completely on a wire rack.

To serve, place the tart pan on top of a large can so that the fluted side falls off. Dust the tart with confectioners' sugar, place it on a platter, and cut it into wedges.

NONNA ANNA'S CIAMBELLA

MAKES ONE 10-INCH BUNDT CAKE

3 CUPS	*all-purpose flour*
2 TABLESPOONS	*baking powder*
4	*large eggs*
I CUP (2 STICKS)	*unsalted butter, at room temperature, plus extra for the pan*
2 CUPS	*sugar*
	Finely grated zest of 1 lemon
PINCH	*salt*
I CUP	*milk*
	KITCHEN STUFF
	Electric mixer
	10-inch Bundt pan

Nonna Anna had the leisure to be somewhat more patient with us kids than my mother; I loved cooking with her. Like my dad, I have a serious sweet tooth and as often as I could, I'd convince her to bake this vanilla-and-lemon-flavored cake with me. It was far and away my favorite thing to do with her.

When I was very young, and too small to reach the counter, she would tie an apron around me and stand me up on a chair so that I could help with the mixing. It was fabulous fun for a seven-year-old! I grated lemon zest, helped stir the batter, and by the time we were done, there was flour absolutely everywhere. It was my first experience with baking (my mother didn't bake much in those days), and I was fascinated by the alchemy of it: you mixed this thing, poured it into a pan, and it emerged from the oven completely transformed into a perfectly molded cake.

But the best part was still to come. After it was baked, I would present the cake to my dad. He loves ciambella. And it delighted my young child self that something I made with my own small, floury hands could make him so very, very happy.

In my family, we don't like rich, gooey desserts—like most Italians, we prefer something with a lighter texture. Ciambella has a light, dry crumb; it's perfect for dunking in the coffee or dessert wine with which it's traditionally served. Whenever life calls for some serious comforting, I make this; it plops me right back into my mother's kitchen with my grandmother, for whom a bit of glorious messiness was par for the course.

PREHEAT THE OVEN to 350°F and center a rack in the oven. Coat a 10-inch Bundt pan with butter and set aside.

In a bowl, sift the flour with the baking powder and set aside.

Separate the egg yolks from the whites.

In a large bowl, beat the butter with the egg yolks with an electric mixer until the mixture turns a pale yellow color, about 3 minutes. Beat in the sugar, lemon zest, and salt until combined. Beat in the flour mixture in three stages. Beat in the milk until smooth.

In a large, clean bowl, beat the egg whites with the electric mixer on medium speed until stiff peaks form when you lift the beater from the bowl. Add about one quarter of the beaten whites to the batter, and stir to blend. Then add the rest of the whites and fold them carefully into the batter. To do this, take a large rubber spatula and cut down through the whites all the way to the bottom of the bowl. Give the bowl a quarter turn, as you lift the batter from the bottom up and over the whites. Cut down again, give the bowl a quarter turn, and lift the batter over the whites. Keep doing this until the whites are entirely incorporated (there may still be some little blobs of white—that's fine).

Pour the batter into the buttered pan and bake until a toothpick comes out clean, 40 to 50 minutes. Let the cake cool 10 minutes in the pan on a wire rack. Then, wearing oven mitts, place the rack upside down on top of the cake and quickly overturn both cake and rack to release the cake. Let it cool completely before cutting it into slices. Serve with coffee or dessert wine, for dunking.

THE TWIST

Here's how I like to separate eggs: Set out three small bowls. Carefully crack an egg over one of the bowls and break the shell in half. Holding one half-shell in each hand, transfer the egg yolk carefully back and forth between the two halves, allowing the white to drop into the bowl, until it has been almost entirely separated from the yolk. Dump the yolk into a second bowl. Pour the white from the first bowl into the third. Now repeat the process all over again for each egg, using the first bowl to catch the white and, once you've been successful, transferring it to the third bowl; this way, if you get some of the yolk into the white, you can toss the problem egg without contaminating the rest of your whites.

PANE DEGLI ANGELI

MAKES ONE 9-INCH CAKE

2 CUPS	*potato starch*
1¾ TABLESPOONS	*baking powder*
1½ CUPS	*sugar*
5	*large eggs*
¾ CUP	*pure olive oil*
	butter, for the pan
	KITCHEN STUFF
	9-inch springform pan
	Electric mixer

The recipe for this fluffy, angel-food-like cake has been in the family forever. It's extremely local, from the town of Torricella del Pizzo in Cremona, where my mother was born. It was made once a year to celebrate the end of the fall grape harvest.

My mother taught me to make it exactly the same way her mother did, except that now we use an electric mixer instead of a handheld whisk. Oh, and my grandmother didn't have an oven—no-one in town did in those days—so the women and children gathered at the bakery to use the baker's oven once he'd closed up shop for the day.

The secret to this cake and the only even vaguely difficult thing about it is all that whisking. The eggs are added to the sugar one by one, and the mixture must be well beaten in between to give the cake its airy texture. What a lot of work it must have been before there were mixers. It took so much whisking, my mom reminds me often, that she had to sit down on the floor, holding the bowl between her knees, to beat the eggs. A supervising adult would come by now and then to check on her progress. She was always hopeful, but inevitably, the response was No! Beat it more!

Beyond eggs, the major ingredients in this cake are potato starch and olive oil. Potato starch is common in Italian cooking but less so here in America; look for it in the section of the grocery store that sells Kosher products. My mother uses "pure" (rather than "extra-virgin") Filippo Berio brand olive oil for this because it has very light flavor. The cake doesn't taste of olive oil at all.

PREHEAT THE OVEN to 350°F and center a rack in the oven. Butter a 9-inch springform pan.

Sift the potato starch with the baking powder into a bowl or onto a sheet of aluminum foil or parchment paper.

Place the sugar in a medium bowl. Crack in one of the eggs. Starting on low, beat the sugar and egg with an electric mixer until well combined. Then raise the speed to medium and beat until the mixture turns a very pale yellow color, 2 to 3 minutes.

Add the second egg, and beat as before, starting on low speed so as not to get batter all over the kitchen, and then on medium, until the mixture returns to the pale, yellow color. Continue in this way to beat in all the eggs.

With the mixer on medium-low, pour in the oil in a thin, constant stream (it's easier if you have someone help you to pour). Beat until combined.

Now add in the dry ingredients, in about 5 batches, beating until the batter is completely combined between additions.

Pour the batter into the pan and tap the pan lightly on the counter to reduce air bubbles. Bake the cake until it is puffed and lightly browned all over the top, and a tester inserted into the center comes out dry, 50 minutes to 1 hour. Cool the cake completely, placing the pan on a wire rack for at least 1 hour. It will settle slightly as it cools. Then remove the pan, cut the cake into wedges, and serve as is or with fresh fruit and whipped cream.

PRACTICALLY INDESTRUCTIBLE
CREAM CHEESE SPONGE CAKE

SERVES 8

½ CUP	cake flour
2½ TABLESPOONS	cornstarch
5 OUNCES	cream cheese, at room temperature
4½ TABLESPOONS	unsalted butter, at room temperature, plus extra for the pan
6	large eggs, at room temperature
½ CUP	heavy cream
I TABLESPOON	pure vanilla extract
	Pinch salt
¼ TEASPOON	cream of tartar
¾ CUP	sugar
	KITCHEN STUFF
	9-inch springform pan

Looking for a change from traditional, dry Italian cakes, my mom and I played around and came up with this moist, airy sponge cake. It tastes like a cheesecake, with the texture of a very moist sponge cake, and it is, as the name suggests, hard to screw up. It's perfectly delicious on its own, but in the summer, it's wonderful with a fruit salad (page 181) or fresh strawberries.

The cream cheese, butter, and eggs *must* be at room temperature. (Whipping egg whites is a cinch if they're at room temperature.) Depending on the temperature of your kitchen, you'll want to set the ingredients out several hours (but one to two hours at most for the eggs) before you make the cake in order to warm them up. If you think of it, just get them out the night before.

ARRANGE A RACK in the lower third of the oven and preheat the oven to 300°F. Place the bottom of a 9-inch springform pan on a sheet of waxed paper and trace around it with a pencil. Cut out the round. Attach the sides to the pan, and butter the sides and bottom. Place the waxed paper round on the bottom and butter that too. Dust the bottom and sides of the pan with flour and shake out the excess. Cut a large piece of aluminum foil; set the pan in the center of the sheet and fold the edges up the sides of the pan so that the seam between the bottom and sides is completely enclosed and the foil comes almost all the way up to the rim. Find a small roasting pan or baking dish large enough hold the pan with a little room around the sides. Set all this aside while you make the batter.

Sift the cake flour with the cornstarch through a fine sieve, into a bowl. Set that aside.

In a large bowl, beat the cream cheese and butter until smooth and creamy.

Separate the eggs, one at a time. Dump the yolk into the bowl with the cream cheese mixture; dump the white into another large bowl you have ready. With an electric mixer, beat the egg yolk into the cream cheese mixture until thoroughly blended and pale yellow in color. Repeat this process until all the eggs have been used. Beat in the cream, vanilla, and salt until lightened in color.

Add the dry ingredients to the cream cheese mixture and beat until combined.

Clean your beaters well. Add the cream of tartar to the bowl with the egg whites and beat to soft peaks. Gradually add the sugar and beat until shiny, stiff peaks form. Add about one quarter of the beaten whites to the cream cheese mixture and stir to blend. Then add the rest of the whites and fold them carefully into the batter (see page 191 for technique).

Pour the batter into the prepared pan. Tap it a couple of times on the countertop to remove air bubbles, and smooth the top with the spatula. Set the pan in the baking dish. Fill a large measuring cup with lukewarm water and carefully pour the water into the baking dish so that it comes about 1 inch up the sides of the pan. Carefully place the dish with the pan in the oven and bake until the cake is risen and lightly browned on the top, and a tester inserted into the center comes out clean, about 1 hour. Carefully remove the pan from the baking dish and set it on a wire rack. Turn off the oven and leave the water-filled baking dish in there until it has cooled—it's very easy to spill when you remove it from the oven!

Chill the cooled cake in the refrigerator. To serve, run a small knife around the edge of the pan to loosen the cake. Release the spring and remove the sides of the pan. Use a spatula to lift the cake off the bottom, peeling off the waxed paper at the same time. Place the cake on a serving platter and cut it into wedges. Cover and refrigerate any leftovers.

ACKNOWLEDGMENTS

ANNA BOIARDI

I would like to sincerely thank the following people for helping to make my vision a reality:

Stephanie—I could not have asked for a better partner. Thank you for your dedication—it's been quite a journey!

Jennifer Levesque and the entire Abrams team—thank you for the opportunity to share my recipes and memories.

Susan Raihofer—thank you for your enthusiasm, advice, and hard work.

Adam Nettler—thank you for being a part of my team.

Ellen Silverman, Pam, and the team—thank you for the beautiful images.

To Ken, Gianna, and Kelli—a BIG thank you for all your help.

Mom—thank you for being by my side every step of the way.

Bobby, Wendy, Alexandra, and Robert—thank you for your love and support.

Uncle Paul and Aunt Marilyn—thank you for preserving our family history in photos.

Lorenzo, Allison, and Brooke—thank you for your integral part in Cucina Academy, and thank you to everyone who has attended.

Thank you to Sue Burke, Becky Niiya, and everyone at ConAgra.

My heartfelt thanks and love to all my friends and family, who support me on a daily basis and who will always have a place to eat! Ali, Shaun, Brandon, Nicole, Peter, and the entire Genetic team, KLS, Camilla, Loren and J.R., Paola, Jen, Tami, Skye, Ali and Jason, Julie, Nonna and PopPop, Scott, Navroz, Killaen, the entire Boiardi and McCue families, the Cuozzo family, Frank and Michele, Celine, Frado, Giada and Veronica, the Zoellners, Juliette and Steven, Mark and Melissa, Kim Miller, Andrew C., Jim Heckler, Lori D., Clelia, Keith, Brandy, and Craig.

And last, to my husband Jack—thank you for all your support, love, ideas, and inspiration, for believing in me. With you, everyday is an adventure—none of this would be possible without you. I love you. xo

STEPHANIE LYNESS

Thanks to David Black, Dave Larabell, and Susan Raihofer at the David Black Agency, who all get it—and me—so well. Thanks to Leslie Stoker, Jennifer Levesque, and all the folks at Abrams for their hard work, and for seeing the possibilities; thanks to Ellen Silverman and her team for a beautiful book. Thanks to my family and friends, who've been eating and talking Italian food for a long, long time now. Thanks to Angela and Joseph Boiardi for making it immensely fun. And finally, thanks to Anna, who found and stayed her course so beautifully.

CONVERSION CHART

WEIGHT EQUIVALENTS: The metric weights given in this chart are not exact equivalents, but have been rounded up or down slightly to make measuring easier.

VOLUME EQUIVALENTS: These are not exact equivalents for American cups and spoons, but have been rounded up or down slightly to make measuring easier.

AVOIRDUPOIS	METRIC
¼ oz	7 g
½ oz	15 g
1 oz	30 g
2 oz	60 g
3 oz	90 g
4 oz	115 g
5 oz	150 g
6 oz	175 g
7 oz	200 g
8 oz (½ lb)	225 g
9 oz	250 g
10 oz	300 g
11 oz	325 g
12 oz	350 g
13 oz	375 g
14 oz	400 g
15 oz	425 g
16 oz (1 lb)	450 g
1½ lb	750 g
2 lb	900 g
2¼ lb	1 kg
3 lb	1.4 kg
4 lb	1.8 kg

AMERICAN	METRIC	IMPERIAL
¼ tsp	1.2 ml	
½ tsp	2.5 ml	
1 tsp	5.0 ml	
½ Tbsp (1.5 tsp)	7.5 ml	
1 Tbsp (3 tsp)	15 ml	
¼ cup (4 Tbsp)	60 ml	2 fl oz
⅓ cup (5 Tbsp)	75 ml	2.5 fl oz
½ cup (8 Tbsp)	125 ml	4 fl oz
⅔ cup (10 Tbsp)	150 ml	5 fl oz
¾ cup (12 Tbsp)	175 ml	6 fl oz
1 cup (16 Tbsp)	250 ml	8 fl oz
1¼ cups	300 ml	10 fl oz (½ pint)
1½ cups	350 ml	12 fl oz
2 cups (1 pint)	500 ml	16 fl oz
2½ cups	625 ml	20 fl oz (1 pint)
1 quart	1 liter	32 fl oz

OVEN MARK	F	C	GAS
Very cool	250–275	130–140	½–1
Cool	300	150	2
Warm	325	170	3
Moderate	350	180	4
Moderately hot	375	190	5
	400	200	6
Hot	425	220	7
	450	230	8
Very hot	475	250	9

INDEX

(PAGE REFERENCES IN *ITALICS* REFER TO ILLUSTRATIONS.)

W

Z

RECIPE INDEX